Justin —

<u>I am</u> forever gratef

in which you have changed my

continue to do so everyday. Thank you

for always showing me the doors available

for me to open, believing in my ability

I AM

A Life-changing Guide to Creating the Future You Desire

to open them, and encouraging me to be

who I truly am. You are an incredible

Janine Naomi Grant

#LaGringa

leader and I am so humbled to have

the opportunity to be on this adventure

with you.

♡ ☺   Janine

7/12/18

ISBN: 1546666036

ISBN-13: 978-1546666035

DEDICATION

I wrote this book for myself, but definitely not by myself.

If you played a role in my life before May 8th 2017 in any way, shape, or form you were a critical part of this book becoming a reality. Thank you. Thank you for your support, your thoughts, your love, your inspiration, and most of all thank you for being you. Without other people we cannot become who we are truly meant to be. Live your life in Ubuntu at all times.

If you're new to my life, welcome! I am excited to have you. And don't worry, you'll be on the dedication page of my second book. ☺

- #LaGringa -

CONTENTS

INTRODUCTION

Dear Friend,

For years my goals and I were two separate things. My goals looked at me from the pages of a journal, and from the images on a vision board. While I could see what I wanted, I did not internally feel in line with them becoming a reality. I felt like I had clarity on what I wanted for my future, yet the speed at which I was approaching those goals was rather sluggish and the vision I had seemed more like someone else's future than my own. Have you ever felt that way before? If so, this book is for you.

Over time from various mentors, gurus, and leaders I learned the power of the two words "I am". For years the ideas and power behind "I am" flirted with me. These two words would come up again and again in my studies asking me to pay attention to them. Then one day, it all finally clicked. Once I learned how to unlock the power of these two words, the weights that held me back lifted and I finally felt in line with the future that I desired. When I started to implement this journal as a daily practice everything changed. Almost immediately after implementing this ritual I started running toward my vision, accomplishing goals along the way. This journal will teach you a practice that it took me years to finally implement and understand. My mission is to help you take the fast track and learn what took me years in just the next few pages.

"I am" are the single two most powerful words in the English language because they shape the constructs of our mind and our perception of self-reality. These two small words and the way in which we use them ultimately determine the way we approach life, challenges, love and the pursuit of our ultimate possibilities. They define what we believe about ourselves. These two words used the wrong way can cause all the problems that consume many lives today and infect our World with self-doubt, envy, fear, hatred, and confusion. However, these two words used with powerful positive intention, can change the World, can change your life, and you can start today.

<u>I am</u> … SO excited for you that you have decided to embark on this journey because it is one that has radically changed my life, and the lives of those around me. I am confident that when you commit to the short but immensely impactful daily practice in this journal, in your daily language, and in your thoughts, that your life will align with your greatest purpose and you will achieve magnificent things.

Love Always,

Janine Naomi Grant

#LaGringa

CHAPTER 1:
THE DAILY PRACTICE OF THE 1%

The quickest way to achieve success is to learn from the people who have already accomplished the goals you've set for yourself. If no one else has accomplished the goals you have, even better, than means you are thinking BIG! Even in that case, you can still learn from those who came close. Finding the people who have already endured the path allows you to fast track the lessons they've learned, the mistakes they've made, and the keys to success that they've discovered. They have already put in hundreds of thousands of hours and thanks to them you don't have to *if* you learn from them and apply their lessons.

Over the past several years I have committed myself to learning about the 1% and discovering what makes them different. Not just in their lifestyle, possessions, and power but in their daily practices and thoughts that consume their minds. While many practices are utilized amongst the World's 1%'ers there is one daily habit that truly permeates the entire group as a key to success. That is the daily practice of writing down their goals.

In my past I had attempted to write out my goals monthly, but more often I ended up writing them down very 3-6 months. Sometimes even only once a year. I would go back and read them every month or so. But more often than not I would write them down once in a journal, close the journal next to my bed, and forget about it until I found myself in a low moment and needed to remember why I was even moving forward in the first place.

I was living my life in waves. I would get inspired, feel motivated, change my habits for a week or two and launch myself towards my goals. Then after just a few days, weeks, or sometimes even just hours, I would go back to what I had done before. Again and again I would find myself back at the starting point. I was like a plane that revved up the engines, began take off and at the first sign of turbulence decided to come in for a landing and return to the gate. I used all my energy to get started, only to give up before I made a breakthrough. I could never get myself to cruising altitude. In fact, I only ever got a few hundred feet off the ground, just enough to see a small glimpse of the view before it all went away again. With my energy depleted, I felt like a failure. I feared that I was destined to stay at the terminal going through the wave of ramp up, take off, get a glimpse, hard landing, and start over for the rest of my life. **But deep down I knew that I was meant to soar, meant to take off to inexplicable heights, and see the universe – <u>and so are YOU</u>!**

My problem was that I didn't know how to break through, and my guess is that if you are reading this you can relate to having that feeling either right now, or in previous times in your life. This journaling practice which you are about to embark on and the understanding of the true power and intentions of the words "I am" have radically changed my life and allowed to me take off on my true journey to new heights every day.

As I continued to learn about the 1% I would hear over and over again the importance of <u>daily</u> journaling, <u>daily</u> reminders of your goals, and <u>daily</u> habits that set these individuals apart. The problem was that DAILY sounded like a lot to me. Daily was a big commitment that I was not willing to keep up with. If you have been reading this so far and thinking "Daily? I have to write in this book EVERY DAY? Can't I just do it every other day, or once a week or something? Will it really matter?" **I can relate, because that's why I put off this practice for so long.**

If you truly want to create lasting change, to achieve all the things in your vision, to check off all the goals on your list, and to live to your true purpose in life, this will need to be a daily practice. As a mentor of mine says, "Anything worth doing, is worth doing every day." **I am guessing you wouldn't be holding this book right now unless you knew that you are capable of achieving more than you have right now.** That potential, that is worth taking time every day to hone and tap into. <u>You are worth it.</u>

The journal included in this book has 365 pages, 1 page for each day of the year. To start I ask that you give yourself a <u>firm</u> commitment that you will find 15 minutes to fit this into your morning routine for the next 30 days, even if that means waking up 15 minutes earlier. There are 3 critical steps which I will explain in chapter 3 to ensure this practice will have its full strength. Done correctly you can fit all 3 steps into just 15 minutes each morning.

So here we go – 30 days straight! No days off, and weekends count. Even if you're on vacation, bring your journal with you. Recently I was on a cruise, and as you can see I brought my journals with me – daily habits mean EVERY day. I can guarantee you once those 30 days go by you'll experience so much impact in your life from this practice that you will never go a morning without it again.

CHAPTER 2:
TWO LIFE-CHANGING WORDS: "I AM"

Every day each of us say hundreds of statements beginning with the words "I am." Pay attention today and you'll hear yourself and those around you constantly defining themselves using these two tiny but mighty words.

I am hungry.

I am good.

I am so stupid.

I am bored.

I am confused.

I am too broke to do that.

I am tired.

Unfortunately, our society has become so accustom to negativity it is more accepted to use "I am" statements to talk about the things that we are unhappy with than that which we are happy with. When you say "I am tired" or "I am broke" you confirm to the World, to yourself, and your subconscious mind that is what you are. Often we do this in jest, or without thinking our words have weight. The truth is the more you say "I am tired" the more you will feel tired. The more you say "I am broke" the more you think and act in agreement with that statement.

Millions of people say negative things about themselves hundreds of times a day and then wonder why they are stuck in the same place feeling a lack of a confidence, unhealthy, demotivated, and financially in a hole. The reason why is that we constantly say statements that are not in accordance with our goals and define to ourselves that is who we are. Your subconscious mind doesn't know the difference between your words and reality, so that starts to become your reality. Think about how often you or people around you have said some of the following statements:

I am bored.

I am ugly.

I am overwhelmed.

I am fat.

I am tired.

I am overworked, and underpaid.

I am broke.

Do you want to be bored? Or feel ugly? Probably not. Yet as part of a cultural norm we say negative things about ourselves without even thinking twice. I challenge you to start examining the statements you say every day and challenge yourself to only say statements that are in unity with what you want. Sometimes this will mean saying the exact opposite of how you actually feel in the moment. For instance, I have implemented this practice when I wake up in the morning. Some days I wake up feeling groggy, and the only thing I am ready to do is turn around and go back to bed. Instead I turn to my puppy and say "Milo, I am full of ENERGY!" I keep repeating it and start to take actions that someone who felt energetic would take. After a few minutes energy starts flowing through my body.

Throughout your day, monitor your language to catch yourself before you say negative "I am" statements that are not in harmony with the life that you want to live. We are all going to have negative feelings and thoughts, and sometimes there is truth there. When you find yourself in a difficult thought that you need to work through remember that momentary feeling does not define who you are. Instead of saying "<u>I am</u> tried" try saying something like, "Right now I feel tired but I am an energetic person!"

When you find yourself saying an "I am" statement that you do not want to align with ask yourself, "How can I feel more in line with the emotions that I *do* want? What would someone that feels the way I want to feel be doing, thinking, and acting right now? Is there someone that felt this way before that got out of it, and can I seek advice from them?" Proactively recognize the I am statements you are using and challenge yourself to rethink the way you are defining yourself and your feelings.

You words <u>do</u> have power, so be cognizant of them and use them for positive change. Forcing yourself to be aware will challenge the way you think, what you say, and the actions you take. As a result your life will change.

The first time I was challenged to do this type of activity was long before I started to study the 1%. I was lost, miserable, anxious, and depressed. As a result of a slow suicide attempt through anorexia, I had landed myself in as an inpatient in a hospital in Philadelphia. I had little confidence, and even less direction. I felt hopeless.

In one of our therapy sessions I was given a journal and told to write down positive things only about myself. I sat staring at the page for a long time without a word written down. I looked up with tears in my eyes explaining that I had nothing to write. My therapist told me to start by writing down things that I liked, telling me to remember who I used to be before I let my depression consume my being and take over my life. I started small and each night I would write down a couple more things. I even drew small illustrations to help my mind absorb the "new" information that had always been there just buried under years of negative mud thrown on top. I was slowly digging myself out and uncovering the greatness that was hidden under all the sludge.

No matter what your starting point is right now, this activity and daily practice will help you to uncover a version of yourself that is far more magnificent than you can envision. You are capable of something so incredibly outstanding that it's impossible for you to even imagine right now.

This is the first page of that journal.

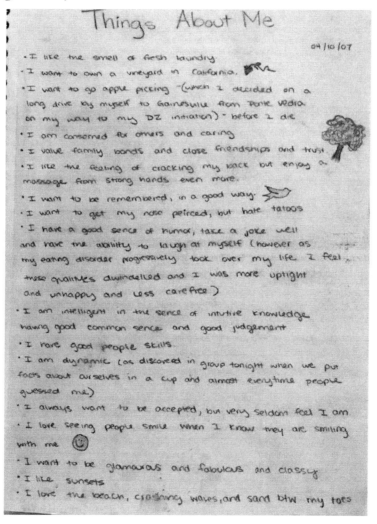

PS. I have since been apple picking, but also got a tattoo.

Along your journey, the biggest challenge will be that the people you surround yourself with may, or more likely may not, adopt this new philosophy with you. I encourage you to surround yourself at your core with people who are like minded, growth oriented, positive people; **your circle of influence will truly change your life.** Encourage them to also get a copy of this journal and put it into practice together.

Regardless of how strong your core circle of influence is, you will interact every day with people who are stuck in a negative "I am" pattern. When you start to say only positive "I am" statements these people will feel uncomfortable, challenged, and even intimidated. In our society today people have the unhealthy habit of connecting and relating to other people's misery and feeling threatened by other's happiness. Your happiness and positivity is not at the expense of anyone else! **There is no scarcity of ability to live the life you want.** In fact, by going after the life you desire at full force you are more likely to help those around you and bring others up than if you give in and decide to relate to their misery. Basking together in a sea of negativity doesn't help either of you to achieve your goals. Stay strong! You can do this. You can create the life you desire, 100% without any exceptions or compromises.

Decide today to stop sending negativity out into the World. The World already has enough of it. Be the person that would and will achieve the goals you set for your life. Be your higher self. **You have permission to let the greatness that is inside of you shine through to the World.** You have the ability to change your life starting at this very instant if you choose to. The only one that can stop you, is you.

Let's start <u>now</u> by writing down 15 positive I am statements that define you. When you write your statements be proud, and be loud about how incredibly amazing you are! **YOU ARE AMAZING it's ok to say so!!!** If you get stuck I've included some pictures of my original "I am Journal" on page 16-20. Feel free to borrow some of your favorite statements or use it for inspiration to come up with your own. You can also write statements that might not be true yet, but that you want to be true, I will explain more about this in the next chapter.

Let's GO! I'll help you start….

I am _____*changing my life starting today*_____

I am _____

I am _____

I am _____

I am _____

I am _____

I am _____

I am _____

I am _____

I am _____

I am _____

I am _____

I am _____

I am _____

I am _____

Congratulations! You've just made a big first step in setting your intentions and being in line with who you truly can be. It may be difficult at first, but it is your responsibility to be your own biggest fan. **You need to give you love.** Never allow yourself to say anything negative about you. Even self-deprecating humor hurts your subconscious and pulls you away from your true self, your greatness, and your purpose in life.

It is normal for people to feel uncomfortable talking positively about themselves at first because of the way our society has shaped our mindsets. The best trick that I have learned to monitor myself talk is to find a photograph of yourself as a small child. As you begin to think or say something negative about yourself that is not in line with you who truly want to be such as…

> I am not smart
>
> I am a loser
>
> I am broke
>
> I am failing at life

… try saying that to the adorable little kid in the photo. "Little Janine, you are not smart, you are a loser, you're broke, and you're failing at life." See it just sounds ridiculous! Why? Because of course it's not true in the first place!!! It's just the B.S. story you have learned to tell yourself overtime. Well, it's time to change that story for good. Follow the 3 steps in the next chapter and you will be on your way to a new positive story and future.

I am happy
I make the world a better place
I am significant
I am relevant
I am rich
I am abundant
I am a light
I am a becon of hope
I am an inspiration
I am tremendously powerful
I am capable
I can do even more than I even think I can
I push my limits and set new standards
I surprise myself
I am a loving mommy to Milo
I am a loving daughter, sister and friend
I am a superstar in my profession
Everyone wants to work with me
I am a magnet for positiviny
I am greatful
I am happy
I am in love
I am abundant

I am confident

I am strong

I am in peak physical shape

I am always improving

I am challengeing myself in positive ways

I am getting better

I have an outstanding life

I am living the life of my dreams

I achieve anything I decide-I want

I am confident

I am enough

I am more than enough

I am legendary

I am making a difference

I am a leader

I am a teacher and coach

I am a business woman

I am a CEO

I am a multipimillionaire

I am a real estate mogule

I am a force for good

I improve peoples lives

I am an inspiration to all those around me

I am full of abundant energy

I am positive and happy

I am a loving caring person

I am in a passionate, loving, trusting rewarding and fulling romantic relationship

I am able to provide my family with the best of the best

I wear Channel and BCBG outfits with designer accessories every day

I am able to spend time having fun and loving my Milo

I have quality loving happy time with both my mom and sister every week

I am a multimillionaire who is earning hundreds of millions a year through multiple streams of income

I am strong

I am powerful

I am capable

I am finding the answers

I am brilliant beyond comparison

I am married to the most incredible man I have ever met, we are madly in love and building an empire together - our relationship grows stronger each and every day

I am in peak physical shape.

I am a force for good in the universe

I am an inspiration to others

I am a Superstar *

I have a Net worth of over $100M and growing daily through multiple streams of income

I am incredible

I am strong

I am an inspiration to others

I own 5000+ rental properties w/
$5M net income a year from that

I am legendary

I am famous for my success and positive
impact that I've made in the world

I am an amazing mommy to Milo

I am a positive force in the universe

I am abundantly happy

I am tremendously in love w/ my husband
and he is the most incredible person
I have ever met

CHAPTER 3:
UNLOCKING THE FULL POWER OF THE JOURNAL ACTIVITY

There are 3 key steps to complete each morning in order to fully unlock the greatness within you and create the future you desire. I am… abundantly confident that if you commit to these 3 steps for a minimum of 15 minutes each morning for the next 30 days straight that the results will be life changing and begin to alter your energy, confidence, and direction in life in such magnitude that you will never go back to life without this practice again.

Step 1: WRITE

The first step is to write down, using the space within this journal, 20 positive statements every morning. They can be the same every morning, or different whatever suits you. The journal makes it turn-key for you with space to write 15 "I am" statements, followed by 5 positive action statements. Here are some examples of each:

"I am" statements:

I am strong

I am powerful

I am abundant

I am a force for good in the universe

I am connected with God

"Positive action statements"

I help others every day.

I love my life.

I aggressively pursue my goals.

One trick is that they don't need to be true yet, they just need to be what you want to be true. For instance I always write some version of my 3 most important goals somewhere in that day's entry. These have not come to fruition yet, but I know that they will.

I am married to the most incredible man in the World and we are abundantly happy, love each other deeply and have a passionate relationship with God as our foundation and our love grows stronger every day. Together we are building and empire and making the World a better place.

I am a multimillionaire with net worth of over $100M and growing.

I travel the World to the most elite destinations with the most powerful, successful, impressive, and inspiring people on the planet.

Writing down your goals in present tense helps you experience the feelings that are associated with the goal actually happening. Switching from saying "I want to…" or "I am going to…" and simply stating your goals as if they have already been achieved will help you to experience the emotions of that goal being real.

If you were to flip through my personal journal you would also find that on certain days I write what I need to hear instead of what I am actually feeling. As an example one morning I was feeling defeated because someone had said some very cruel things to me that left me feeling very lonely, confused, and unconfident in my actions. As a result I needed to re-set my thoughts so here is what I wrote down:

> People love me
> I am a kind and generous person that treats others with respect
> I am full of positive energy that radiates to those around me
> I am an abundant source for good in the universe and I help people everyday
> I am fulfilling my true calling in life
> I actively pursue growth
> I challenge myself daily
> I read 60+ books a year
> I challenge myself to improve everyday
> I face all my challenges with a positive attitude and dominate my fears
> I inspire those around me
> I bring in millions of $ in income annually
> My net worth is over $100M
> I identify and conquer my limiting beliefs, fears, and whats holding me back
> I have a mentor who I work closely with and propells me to greater heights
> I never quit on my goals

Remember, you do not have to accept other people's guilt, thoughts or negative opinions. Those things are a reflection of them not you.

As you sit down to write each morning try to do so in a place that makes you feel happy. Personally I like to sit out on my balcony, or in a small garden outside of my office. I feel most connected to God and to my higher purpose when I am outside, so that is what works best for me. Another good technique to get in a positive mindset before you write is to listen to music that makes you feel motivated. I created a special playlist on my phone called my "state-change" playlist that is a compilation of songs that have the ability to pull me from a negative mindset to a positive one.

Step 2: RECITE

Once you have written down your 15 "I am" statements and 5 positive action statements, it is time it time to make them more permanent in your mind by reading them out loud. Usually I read mine to my puppy Milo, sometimes just to myself. As you read them out loud, read them with declaration and purpose. Own each statement as if it were 100% true, because it is! FEEL the force behind the words, and the joy that comes with embodying them. This might feel a little goofy at first, that's ok! **Feel the awkwardness, and do it anyway.**

At the very least recite your list directly after writing it in the morning. If you want to really bring this to the next level keep your list with you throughout the day and repeat it midday, in the evening, and any time that you feel self-doubt, or negativity creeping in.

Step 3: LIGHT the World on FIRE with your passion

The third step in this equation is to use those words to light your internal flame. Feel the power behind the positive statements and live your day in accordance to what you write down each morning. As you go about your day repeat your affirmations to yourself, feel the strength behind the positive truth, and let it guide you through your challenges. Be proud of who you are, and own the "I am" statements that you write down each morning with confidence.

Every moment of the day embody the words that you write down on the page. **Be the person that you want to become. The only one stopping you, is you. You can be all that you want to be every day. In fact, you already are, you've just been hiding it from yourself and from the World.**

One of my favorite examples of this came from a best friend of mine. After recently introducing her to the "I am" concept she went on a run with a good friend who was a more experienced and avid runner than herself. About two thirds through the run she felt like she may not be able to continue. She started to repeat to herself "I am strong. My legs are powerful. I am going to complete this run. I am a runner. I am strong. I am strong." Through lighting her internal fire, and connecting with positive "I am" statements she was able to not only complete the run, but also prove to herself that she was more capable than she previously thought.

You are an incredible force in the universe, you are capable of more than you can imagine right now, and you can creative positive change in your life and in the lives of others.

NOW it's time to go do it! Let's begin!!!

"It's not selfish to go after what you want, it's brave." - #LaGringa

Day 1:   Today's Date: ___/___/____

I am _____

I am _____

I am _____

I am _____

I am _____

I am _____

I am _____

I am _____

I am _____

I am _____

I am _____

I am _____

I am _____

I am _____

I am _____

I _____

I _____

I _____

I _____

I _____

"Never make the minimum payment in life, how you do one thing is how you do everything." - #LaGringa

Day 2:   Today's Date: ___/___/____

I am _____

I am _____

I am _____

I am _____

I am _____

I am _____

I am _____

I am _____

I am _____

I am _____

I am _____

I am _____

I am _____

I am _____

I am _____

I _____

I _____

I _____

I _____

I _____

"Be BOLD. Ask tough questions. Separate yourself. YOU are different." - #LaGringa

Day 3:   Today's Date: ___/___/____

I am _____

I am _____

I am _____

I am _____

I am _____

I am _____

I am _____

I am _____

I am _____

I am _____

I am _____

I am _____

I am _____

I am _____

I am _____

I _____

I _____

I _____

I _____

I _____

"If you don't take risks, you will always envy those who do." - #LaGringa

Day 4:   Today's Date: ___/___/____

I am _____

I am _____

I am _____

I am _____

I am _____

I am _____

I am _____

I am _____

I am _____

I am _____

I am _____

I am _____

I am _____

I am _____

I am _____

I _____

I _____

I _____

I _____

I _____

"When I take all the shots I have because I am willing to loose and start over, I end up winning more." - #LaGringa

Day 5:   Today's Date: ___/___/____

I am _____

I am _____

I am _____

I am _____

I am _____

I am _____

I am _____

I am _____

I am _____

I am _____

I am _____

I am _____

I am _____

I am _____

I am _____

I _____

I _____

I _____

I _____

I _____

"Live RICH $$$" - #LaGringa

Day 6:   Today's Date: ___/___/____

I am _____

I am _____

I am _____

I am _____

I am _____

I am _____

I am _____

I am _____

I am _____

I am _____

I am _____

I am _____

I am _____

I am _____

I am _____

I _____

I _____

I _____

I _____

I _____

"You need to sow BEFORE you can reap. Stop asking where it is and GO GET IT." – #LaGringa

Day 7:   Today's Date: ___/___/____

I am _____

I am _____

I am _____

I am _____

I am _____

I am _____

I am _____

I am _____

I am _____

I am _____

I am _____

I am _____

I am _____

I am _____

I am _____

I _____

I _____

I _____

I _____

I _____

"Instead of looking for what you want, BECOME who you want and what you want will align with you." - #LaGringa

Day 8:   Today's Date: ___/___/___

I am _____

I am _____

I am _____

I am _____

I am _____

I am _____

I am _____

I am _____

I am _____

I am _____

I am _____

I am _____

I am _____

I am _____

I am _____

I am _____

I _____

I _____

I _____

I _____

I _____

"What will your view from the top look like?" - #LaGringa

Day 9: Today's Date: ___/___/____

I am _____

I am _____

I am _____

I am _____

I am _____

I am _____

I am _____

I am _____

I am _____

I am _____

I am _____

I am _____

I am _____

I am _____

I am _____

I _____

I _____

I _____

I _____

I _____

"What inspires you?" - #LaGringa

Day 10: Today's Date: ___/___/____

I am _____

I am _____

I am _____

I am _____

I am _____

I am _____

I am _____

I am _____

I am _____

I am _____

I am _____

I am _____

I am _____

I am _____

I am _____

I _____

I _____

I _____

I _____

I _____

"Write your future in order to achieve your future." - #LaGringa

Day 11: Today's Date: ___/___/____

I am _____

I am _____

I am _____

I am _____

I am _____

I am _____

I am _____

I am _____

I am _____

I am _____

I am _____

I am _____

I am _____

I am _____

I am _____

I _____

I _____

I _____

I _____

I _____

"What goal do you have that scares you most? Why?" - #LaGringa

Day 12: Today's Date: ___/___/____

I am _____

I am _____

I am _____

I am _____

I am _____

I am _____

I am _____

I am _____

I am _____

I am _____

I am _____

I am _____

I am _____

I am _____

I am _____

I _____

I _____

I _____

I _____

I _____

"Winning does matter." - #LaGringa

Day 13: Today's Date: ___/___/____

I am _____

I am _____

I am _____

I am _____

I am _____

I am _____

I am _____

I am _____

I am _____

I am _____

I am _____

I am _____

I am _____

I am _____

I am _____

I _____

I _____

I _____

I _____

I _____

"What makes you stronger?" - #LaGringa

Day 14: Today's Date: ___/___/____

I am _____

I am _____

I am _____

I am _____

I am _____

I am _____

I am _____

I am _____

I am _____

I am _____

I am _____

I am _____

I am _____

I am _____

I am _____

I _____

I _____

I _____

I _____

I _____

"Tus metas son importantes." - #LaGringa

Day 15: Today's Date: ___/___/____

I am _____

I am _____

I am _____

I am _____

I am _____

I am _____

I am _____

I am _____

I am _____

I am _____

I am _____

I am _____

I am _____

I am _____

I am _____

I _____

I _____

I _____

I _____

I _____

"You deserve it." - #LaGringa

Day 16: Today's Date: ___/___/____

I am _____

I am _____

I am _____

I am _____

I am _____

I am _____

I am _____

I am _____

I am _____

I am _____

I am _____

I am _____

I am _____

I am _____

I am _____

I _____

I _____

I _____

I _____

I _____

"Be the best version of yourself, everyday." - #LaGringa

Day 17: Today's Date: ___/___/____

I am _____

I am _____

I am _____

I am _____

I am _____

I am _____

I am _____

I am _____

I am _____

I am _____

I am _____

I am _____

I am _____

I am _____

I am _____

I _____

I _____

I _____

I _____

I _____

"See the WORLD." - #LaGringa

Day 18: Today's Date: ___/___/____

I am _____

I am _____

I am _____

I am _____

I am _____

I am _____

I am _____

I am _____

I am _____

I am _____

I am _____

I am _____

I am _____

I am _____

I am _____

I _____

I _____

I _____

I _____

I _____

"Defy Definition." - #LaGringa

Day 19: Today's Date: ___/___/____

I am _____

I am _____

I am _____

I am _____

I am _____

I am _____

I am _____

I am _____

I am _____

I am _____

I am _____

I am _____

I am _____

I am _____

I am _____

I _____

I _____

I _____

I _____

I _____

"Be your own biggest fan – support yourself." - #LaGringa

Day 20: Today's Date: ___/___/____

I am _____

I am _____

I am _____

I am _____

I am _____

I am _____

I am _____

I am _____

I am _____

I am _____

I am _____

I am _____

I am _____

I am _____

I am _____

I _____

I _____

I _____

I _____

I _____

"Every day take one step in the direction of your goals." - #LaGringa

Day 21: Today's Date: ___/___/____

I am _____

I am _____

I am _____

I am _____

I am _____

I am _____

I am _____

I am _____

I am _____

I am _____

I am _____

I am _____

I am _____

I am _____

I am _____

I am _____

I _____

I _____

I _____

I _____

I _____

"Never doubt yourself or your vision." - #LaGringa

Day 22: Today's Date: ___/___/____

I am _____

I am _____

I am _____

I am _____

I am _____

I am _____

I am _____

I am _____

I am _____

I am _____

I am _____

I am _____

I am _____

I am _____

I am _____

I _____

I _____

I _____

I _____

I _____

"Impossible goals can become possible." - #LaGringa

Day 23: Today's Date: ___/___/____

I am _____

I am _____

I am _____

I am _____

I am _____

I am _____

I am _____

I am _____

I am _____

I am _____

I am _____

I am _____

I am _____

I am _____

I am _____

I _____

I _____

I _____

I _____

I _____

"If you were a boss, would you hire you." - #LaGringa

Day 24: Today's Date: ___/___/____

I am _____

I am _____

I am _____

I am _____

I am _____

I am _____

I am _____

I am _____

I am _____

I am _____

I am _____

I am _____

I am _____

I am _____

I am _____

I _____

I _____

I _____

I _____

I _____

"Put on a playlist that makes you dance!" - #LaGringa

Day 25: Today's Date: ___/___/____

I am _____

I am _____

I am _____

I am _____

I am _____

I am _____

I am _____

I am _____

I am _____

I am _____

I am _____

I am _____

I am _____

I am _____

I am _____

I _____

I _____

I _____

I _____

I _____

"I still believe in fairytales." - #LaGringa

Day 26: Today's Date: ___/___/____

I am _____

I am _____

I am _____

I am _____

I am _____

I am _____

I am _____

I am _____

I am _____

I am _____

I am _____

I am _____

I am _____

I am _____

I am _____

I am _____

I _____

I _____

I _____

I _____

I _____

"Siempre llega a las estrellas." - #LaGringa

Day 27: Today's Date: ___/___/____

I am _____

I am _____

I am _____

I am _____

I am _____

I am _____

I am _____

I am _____

I am _____

I am _____

I am _____

I am _____

I am _____

I am _____

I am _____

I am _____

I _____

I _____

I _____

I _____

I _____

"When you have a goal… be SPECIFIC." - #LaGringa

Day 28: Today's Date: ___/___/____

I am _____

I am _____

I am _____

I am _____

I am _____

I am _____

I am _____

I am _____

I am _____

I am _____

I am _____

I am _____

I am _____

I am _____

I am _____

I _____

I _____

I _____

I _____

I _____

"Decide its possible. Commit to doing it. Take MASSIVE action." - #LaGringa

Day 29: Today's Date: ___/___/____

I am _____

I am _____

I am _____

I am _____

I am _____

I am _____

I am _____

I am _____

I am _____

I am _____

I am _____

I am _____

I am _____

I am _____

I am _____

I _____

I _____

I _____

I _____

I _____

"Today, you deserve chocolate!" - #LaGringa

Day 30: Today's Date: ___/___/____

I am _____

I am _____

I am _____

I am _____

I am _____

I am _____

I am _____

I am _____

I am _____

I am _____

I am _____

I am _____

I am _____

I am _____

I am _____

I _____

I _____

I _____

I _____

I _____

"Live your life in 90 day runs, with 30 day challenges to keep it interesting." #LaGringa

CONGRATULATIONS!!!
YOU FRICKEN ROCK!!!!!!

You've completed your first 30 day challenge of committing to I am statements every morning! Take some time to reflect. Recognizing your growth and being intentional in your plans will help you to get the most out of this practice!

Did you WRITE every day? _____

Did you RECITE every day? _____

Did you LIGHT the World on fire every day? _____

Which of these three steps could you improve most in? How will you implement that moving forward?

What has changed for you over the past 30 days? What progress have you made? (Tip: Compare your first few journal entries to you most recent)

What would you like to get out of the NEXT 30 days?

You ready to take it from 0 – 60???? REAL QUICK. Let's jump on board for another 30 day challenge and take it to 60 days ☺ YOU GOT THIS.

"You can impact the entire World even if it is just one person at a time."

#LaGringa

STOP and fill out this page BEFORE moving forward.
Has this practice been impactful for you in the last 30 days?
(circle one)

YES   No   YES   Maybe   YES

If you circled YES… HECK YEAH!!! GO YOU!!!! Now it is time to pay it forward. You found out about this book because SOMEONE shared it, and it is changing your life. That means you have the power to change other people's lives simply by sharing this book with them!!!! It is time to impact the WORLD.

Who are 5 people in your life that you think could benefit from this practice?
1. _____
2. _____
3. _____
4. _____
5. _____

What can you do to make sure that they get a new copy of this journal in the next 10 days?
Meet up for coffee and explain to them how much this has impacted you
Send them a link to purchase the book on Amazon
Post it on Social media and tag them
Send them a text message about how impactful it has been for you
Hand write a letter to them about the impact and send it in the mail
Purchase them a copy as a gift

If you circled Maybe…
Have you honestly committed EVERY morning for 30 days straight?
What is causing you to waiver in your feelings towards this daily practice?
What could YOU do to turn your answer into a YES?

If you circled No…
Have you honestly committed EVERY morning for 30 days straight?
What about the exercise is making you feel uncomfortable?
How could you turn it around and make it impact the NEXT 30 days of your life?

"What IF… tomorrow you woke up BEFORE the sun?." - #LaGringa

Day 31: Today's Date: ___/___/____

I am _____

I am _____

I am _____

I am _____

I am _____

I am _____

I am _____

I am _____

I am _____

I am _____

I am _____

I am _____

I am _____

I am _____

I am _____

I am _____

I _____

I _____

I _____

I _____

I _____

"If someone read your mind, would you be proud of what they saw?" - #LaGringa

Day 32: Today's Date: ___/___/____

I am _____

I am _____

I am _____

I am _____

I am _____

I am _____

I am _____

I am _____

I am _____

I am _____

I am _____

I am _____

I am _____

I am _____

I am _____

I _____

I _____

I _____

I _____

I _____

"Respecto, honestidad, comunicación." - #LaGringa

Day 33: Today's Date: ___/___/___

I am _____

I am _____

I am _____

I am _____

I am _____

I am _____

I am _____

I am _____

I am _____

I am _____

I am _____

I am _____

I am _____

I am _____

I am _____

I _____

I _____

I _____

I _____

I _____

"Love YOURSELF first." - #LaGringa

Day 34: Today's Date: ___/___/____

I am _____

I am _____

I am _____

I am _____

I am _____

I am _____

I am _____

I am _____

I am _____

I am _____

I am _____

I am _____

I am _____

I am _____

I am _____

I _____

I _____

I _____

I _____

I _____

"Don't just get fit for the summer, get healthy for life." - #LaGringa

Day 35: Today's Date: ___/___/____

I am _____

I am _____

I am _____

I am _____

I am _____

I am _____

I am _____

I am _____

I am _____

I am _____

I am _____

I am _____

I am _____

I am _____

I am _____

I _____

I _____

I _____

I _____

I _____

"Let go of guilt, it doesn't serve you. Forgive yourself. Move forward, take the actions that you want to now." - #LaGringa

Day 36: Today's Date: ___/___/____

I am _____

I am _____

I am _____

I am _____

I am _____

I am _____

I am _____

I am _____

I am _____

I am _____

I am _____

I am _____

I am _____

I am _____

I am _____

I _____

I _____

I _____

I _____

I _____

"If you could accomplish ONE THING that would immediately improve your life what would it be?" - #LaGringa

Day 37: Today's Date: ___/___/____

I am _____

I am _____

I am _____

I am _____

I am _____

I am _____

I am _____

I am _____

I am _____

I am _____

I am _____

I am _____

I am _____

I am _____

I am _____

I _____

I _____

I _____

I _____

I _____

"Drink juice out of a wine glass #youfancyhuh." - #LaGringa

Day 38: Today's Date: ___/___/____

I am _____

I am _____

I am _____

I am _____

I am _____

I am _____

I am _____

I am _____

I am _____

I am _____

I am _____

I am _____

I am _____

I am _____

I am _____

I _____

I _____

I _____

I _____

I _____

"If it doesn't fit, don't force it." - #LaGringa

Day 39: Today's Date: ___/___/____

I am _____

I am _____

I am _____

I am _____

I am _____

I am _____

I am _____

I am _____

I am _____

I am _____

I am _____

I am _____

I am _____

I am _____

I am _____

I _____

I _____

I _____

I _____

I _____

"Be a master of your time." - #LaGringa

Day 40: Today's Date: ___/___/____

I am _____

I am _____

I am _____

I am _____

I am _____

I am _____

I am _____

I am _____

I am _____

I am _____

I am _____

I am _____

I am _____

I am _____

I am _____

I _____

I _____

I _____

I _____

I _____

"Challenge yourself to do something different today." - #LaGringa

Day 41: Today's Date: ___/___/____

I am _____

I am _____

I am _____

I am _____

I am _____

I am _____

I am _____

I am _____

I am _____

I am _____

I am _____

I am _____

I am _____

I am _____

I am _____

I _____

I _____

I _____

I _____

I _____

"Who you are doesn't have to be who you become." - #LaGringa

Day 42: Today's Date: ___/___/____

I am _____

I am _____

I am _____

I am _____

I am _____

I am _____

I am _____

I am _____

I am _____

I am _____

I am _____

I am _____

I am _____

I am _____

I am _____

I _____

I _____

I _____

I _____

I _____

"Embrace change – it's an excellent thing!" - #LaGringa

Day 43: Today's Date: ___/___/____

I am _____

I am _____

I am _____

I am _____

I am _____

I am _____

I am _____

I am _____

I am _____

I am _____

I am _____

I am _____

I am _____

I am _____

I am _____

I _____

I _____

I _____

I _____

I _____

"Stop compromising your standards. You CAN have it all." - #LaGringa

Day 44: Today's Date: ___/___/____

I am _____

I am _____

I am _____

I am _____

I am _____

I am _____

I am _____

I am _____

I am _____

I am _____

I am _____

I am _____

I am _____

I am _____

I am _____

I _____

I _____

I _____

I _____

I _____

"Tu sonrisa es extremadamente hermosa"- #LaGringa

Day 45: Today's Date: ___/___/____

I am _____

I am _____

I am _____

I am _____

I am _____

I am _____

I am _____

I am _____

I am _____

I am _____

I am _____

I am _____

I am _____

I am _____

I am _____

I _____

I _____

I _____

I _____

I _____

"Never apologize for being you. YOU are INCREDIBLE."- #LaGringa

Day 46: Today's Date: ___/___/____

I am _____

I am _____

I am _____

I am _____

I am _____

I am _____

I am _____

I am _____

I am _____

I am _____

I am _____

I am _____

I am _____

I am _____

I am _____

I _____

I _____

I _____

I _____

I _____

"Take the breaks out, DON"T STOP"- #LaGringa

Day 47: Today's Date: ___/___/____

I am _____

I am _____

I am _____

I am _____

I am _____

I am _____

I am _____

I am _____

I am _____

I am _____

I am _____

I am _____

I am _____

I am _____

I am _____

I am _____

I _____

I _____

I _____

I _____

I _____

"Be with someone that supports you 100% and you support 100%. Then impact the WORLD together." - #LaGringa

Day 48: Today's Date: ___/___/____

I am _____

I am _____

I am _____

I am _____

I am _____

I am _____

I am _____

I am _____

I am _____

I am _____

I am _____

I am _____

I am _____

I am _____

I am _____

I _____

I _____

I _____

I _____

I _____

"Make it your mission to make at least 10 people smile today!" - #LaGringa

Day 49: Today's Date: ___/___/____

I am _____

I am _____

I am _____

I am _____

I am _____

I am _____

I am _____

I am _____

I am _____

I am _____

I am _____

I am _____

I am _____

I am _____

I am _____

I _____

I _____

I _____

I _____

I _____

"A confused mind always says no. Be crystal clear." - #LaGringa

Day 50: Today's Date: ___/___/____

I am _____

I am _____

I am _____

I am _____

I am _____

I am _____

I am _____

I am _____

I am _____

I am _____

I am _____

I am _____

I am _____

I am _____

I am _____

I am _____

I _____

I _____

I _____

I _____

I _____

"Forgive your haters, and hope they find happiness." - #LaGringa

Day 51: Today's Date: ___/___/____

I am _____

I am _____

I am _____

I am _____

I am _____

I am _____

I am _____

I am _____

I am _____

I am _____

I am _____

I am _____

I am _____

I am _____

I am _____

I _____

I _____

I _____

I _____

I _____

"No pierdas tiempo." - #LaGringa

Day 52: Today's Date: ___/___/____

I am _____

I am _____

I am _____

I am _____

I am _____

I am _____

I am _____

I am _____

I am _____

I am _____

I am _____

I am _____

I am _____

I am _____

I am _____

I _____

I _____

I _____

I _____

I _____

"How do YOU define happiness?"- #LaGringa

Day 53: Today's Date: ___/___/____

I am _____

I am _____

I am _____

I am _____

I am _____

I am _____

I am _____

I am _____

I am _____

I am _____

I am _____

I am _____

I am _____

I am _____

I am _____

I _____

I _____

I _____

I _____

I _____

"You don't have to love me. I LOVE ME."- #LaGringa

Day 54: Today's Date: ___/___/____

I am _____

I am _____

I am _____

I am _____

I am _____

I am _____

I am _____

I am _____

I am _____

I am _____

I am _____

I am _____

I am _____

I am _____

I am _____

I _____

I _____

I _____

I _____

I _____

"I am full of energy!!@$&% I am a human espresso bean!" - #LaGringa

Day 55: Today's Date: ___/___/____

I am _____

I am _____

I am _____

I am _____

I am _____

I am _____

I am _____

I am _____

I am _____

I am _____

I am _____

I am _____

I am _____

I am _____

I am _____

I _____

I _____

I _____

I _____

I _____

"True friendship is when someone gives you their marshmallows before leaving the campgrounds." - #LaGringa

Day 56: Today's Date: ___/___/____

I am _____

I am _____

I am _____

I am _____

I am _____

I am _____

I am _____

I am _____

I am _____

I am _____

I am _____

I am _____

I am _____

I am _____

I am _____

I _____

I _____

I _____

I _____

I _____

"Sometimes you can't see what that you're looking directly at." - #LaGringa

Day 57: Today's Date: ___/___/____

I am _____

I am _____

I am _____

I am _____

I am _____

I am _____

I am _____

I am _____

I am _____

I am _____

I am _____

I am _____

I am _____

I am _____

I am _____

I _____

I _____

I _____

I _____

I _____

"Decide exactly what you want or you'll settle for what you don't." - #LaGringa

Day 58: Today's Date: ___/___/_____

I am _____

I am _____

I am _____

I am _____

I am _____

I am _____

I am _____

I am _____

I am _____

I am _____

I am _____

I am _____

I am _____

I am _____

I am _____

I _____

I _____

I _____

I _____

I _____

"You CAN achieve exactly what you want, when you decide not to accept anything less than that." - #LaGringa

Day 59: Today's Date: ___/___/____

I am _____

I am _____

I am _____

I am _____

I am _____

I am _____

I am _____

I am _____

I am _____

I am _____

I am _____

I am _____

I am _____

I am _____

I am _____

I am _____

I _____

I _____

I _____

I _____

I _____

"Eat clean. Stay fit. Be energized!" - #LaGringa

Day 60: Today's Date: ___/___/____

I am _____

I am _____

I am _____

I am _____

I am _____

I am _____

I am _____

I am _____

I am _____

I am _____

I am _____

I am _____

I am _____

I am _____

I am _____

I _____

I _____

I _____

I _____

I _____

"Estoy orgulloso de ti"

-#LaGringa

CONGRATULATIONS!!!

LOOK AT YOU GO!!!! ROCKING IT!!!

You've completed your SECOND 30 day challenge of committing to I am statements every morning! That's right, you are a ROCKSTAR! Take some time to reflect. Recognizing your growth and being intentional in your plans will help you to get the most out of this practice!

On Days 31 – 60…

Did you WRITE every day? _____

Did you RECITE every day? _____

Did you LIGHT the World on fire every day? _____

Which of these three steps could you improve most in? How will you implement that moving forward?

What has changed for you over the past 30 days? What progress have you made? (Tip: Compare your day 30/31/32 journal entries to you most recent)

What would you like to get out of the <u>NEXT</u> 30 days?

Let's go BIG – up to the 90 Day BENCHMARK!

"There is no benefit of acting smaller so that those around you feel more comfortable. Share your BIG goals. Be LOUD about it!!" - #LaGringa

Day 61: Today's Date: ___/___/____

I am _____

I am _____

I am _____

I am _____

I am _____

I am _____

I am _____

I am _____

I am _____

I am _____

I am _____

I am _____

I am _____

I am _____

I am _____

I _____

I _____

I _____

I _____

I _____

"I won't live forever but my influence and legacy can." - #LaGringa

Day 62: Today's Date: ___/___/____

I am _____

I am _____

I am _____

I am _____

I am _____

I am _____

I am _____

I am _____

I am _____

I am _____

I am _____

I am _____

I am _____

I am _____

I am _____

I am _____

I _____

I _____

I _____

I _____

I _____

"Your mind is powerful. Do you expect haters or do you expect RAVING fans? Maybe it's just in your head…" - #LaGringa

Day 63: Today's Date: ___/___/____

I am _____

I am _____

I am _____

I am _____

I am _____

I am _____

I am _____

I am _____

I am _____

I am _____

I am _____

I am _____

I am _____

I am _____

I am _____

I _____

I _____

I _____

I _____

I _____

"The answer lies within you." - #LaGringa

Day 64: Today's Date: ___/___/____

I am _____

I am _____

I am _____

I am _____

I am _____

I am _____

I am _____

I am _____

I am _____

I am _____

I am _____

I am _____

I am _____

I am _____

I am _____

I _____

I _____

I _____

I _____

I _____

"I don't have to smoke, I'm already high." - #LaGringa

Day 65: Today's Date: ___/___/____

I am _____

I am _____

I am _____

I am _____

I am _____

I am _____

I am _____

I am _____

I am _____

I am _____

I am _____

I am _____

I am _____

I am _____

I am _____

I am _____

I _____

I _____

I _____

I _____

I _____

"Become the type of person that you would want to surround yourself with and you will start attracting them into your life." - #LaGringa

Day 66: Today's Date: ___/___/____

I am _____

I am _____

I am _____

I am _____

I am _____

I am _____

I am _____

I am _____

I am _____

I am _____

I am _____

I am _____

I am _____

I am _____

I am _____

I _____

I _____

I _____

I _____

I _____

"What phone call could you make right NOW that could alter the course of your life forever? DO IT." - #LaGringa

Day 67: Today's Date: ___/___/____

I am _____

I am _____

I am _____

I am _____

I am _____

I am _____

I am _____

I am _____

I am _____

I am _____

I am _____

I am _____

I am _____

I am _____

I am _____

I _____

I _____

I _____

I _____

I _____

"Turns out things that are extremely difficult become abundantly easy when you just DECIDE that you're doing to do them." - #LaGringa

Day 68: Today's Date: ___/___/____

I am _____

I am _____

I am _____

I am _____

I am _____

I am _____

I am _____

I am _____

I am _____

I am _____

I am _____

I am _____

I am _____

I am _____

I am _____

I _____

I _____

I _____

I _____

I _____

"I won't live forever but my influence and legacy can." - #LaGringa

Day 69: Today's Date: ___/___/____

I am _____

I am _____

I am _____

I am _____

I am _____

I am _____

I am _____

I am _____

I am _____

I am _____

I am _____

I am _____

I am _____

I am _____

I am _____

I _____

I _____

I _____

I _____

I _____

"There is no future, there is only NOW. LIVE IT." - #LaGringa

Day 70: Today's Date: ___/___/____

I am _____

I am _____

I am _____

I am _____

I am _____

I am _____

I am _____

I am _____

I am _____

I am _____

I am _____

I am _____

I am _____

I am _____

I am _____

I _____

I _____

I _____

I _____

I _____

"Never show up empty handed." - #LaGringa

Day 71: Today's Date: ___/___/____

I am _____

I am _____

I am _____

I am _____

I am _____

I am _____

I am _____

I am _____

I am _____

I am _____

I am _____

I am _____

I am _____

I am _____

I am _____

I _____

I _____

I _____

I _____

I _____

"Vives su vida!" - #LaGringa

Day 72: Today's Date: ___/___/____

I am _____

I am _____

I am _____

I am _____

I am _____

I am _____

I am _____

I am _____

I am _____

I am _____

I am _____

I am _____

I am _____

I am _____

I am _____

I _____

I _____

I _____

I _____

I _____

"Clean up your life." - #LaGringa

Day 73: Today's Date: ___/___/___

I am _____

I am _____

I am _____

I am _____

I am _____

I am _____

I am _____

I am _____

I am _____

I am _____

I am _____

I am _____

I am _____

I am _____

I am _____

I am _____

I _____

I _____

I _____

I _____

I _____

"There is a massive difference between a princess and a Queen or a prince and a King. Which one are you? Do your actions show it?" - #LaGringa

Day 74: Today's Date: ___/___/____

I am _____

I am _____

I am _____

I am _____

I am _____

I am _____

I am _____

I am _____

I am _____

I am _____

I am _____

I am _____

I am _____

I am _____

I am _____

I _____

I _____

I _____

I _____

I _____

"Staying where you are might FEEL safe, but the reality is not moving is the most dangerous move you have." - #LaGringa

Day 75: Today's Date: ___/___/____

I am _____

I am _____

I am _____

I am _____

I am _____

I am _____

I am _____

I am _____

I am _____

I am _____

I am _____

I am _____

I am _____

I am _____

I am _____

I _____

I _____

I _____

I _____

I _____

"Just be YOU. Everyone else is taken. You are AWESOME!!!" - #LaGringa

Day 76: Today's Date: ___/___/____

I am _____

I am _____

I am _____

I am _____

I am _____

I am _____

I am _____

I am _____

I am _____

I am _____

I am _____

I am _____

I am _____

I am _____

I am _____

I _____

I _____

I _____

I _____

I _____

"Enamórate de ti mismo." - #LaGringa

Day 77: Today's Date: ___/___/____

I am _____

I am _____

I am _____

I am _____

I am _____

I am _____

I am _____

I am _____

I am _____

I am _____

I am _____

I am _____

I am _____

I am _____

I _____

I _____

I _____

I _____

I _____

"Never succumb to the danger of commonality. Be different." - #LaGringa

Day 78: Today's Date: ___/___/____

I am _____

I am _____

I am _____

I am _____

I am _____

I am _____

I am _____

I am _____

I am _____

I am _____

I am _____

I am _____

I am _____

I am _____

I am _____

I am _____

I _____

I _____

I _____

I _____

I _____

"Be intentional about what breakthroughs you want in your life. Choose your future with your thoguhts." - #LaGringa

Day 79: Today's Date: ___/___/___

I am _____

I am _____

I am _____

I am _____

I am _____

I am _____

I am _____

I am _____

I am _____

I am _____

I am _____

I am _____

I am _____

I am _____

I am _____

I _____

I _____

I _____

I _____

I _____

"When you walk in, is the room better for it?" - #LaGringa

Day 80: Today's Date: ___/___/____

I am _____

I am _____

I am _____

I am _____

I am _____

I am _____

I am _____

I am _____

I am _____

I am _____

I am _____

I am _____

I am _____

I am _____

I am _____

I _____

I _____

I _____

I _____

I _____

"There is someone that needs to hear what you have to say. Share your story with the entire World. You could be helping that person right now!" - #LaGringa

Day 81: Today's Date: ___/___/____

I am _____

I am _____

I am _____

I am _____

I am _____

I am _____

I am _____

I am _____

I am _____

I am _____

I am _____

I am _____

I am _____

I am _____

I am _____

I _____

I _____

I _____

I _____

I _____

"Redefine what an emergency is, and set clear boundaries." - #LaGringa

Day 82: Today's Date: ___/___/____

I am _____

I am _____

I am _____

I am _____

I am _____

I am _____

I am _____

I am _____

I am _____

I am _____

I am _____

I am _____

I am _____

I am _____

I am _____

I _____

I _____

I _____

I _____

I _____

"It's worth it to weather through uncertainty. You are worth it."- #LaGringa

Day 83: Today's Date: ___/___/____

I am _____

I am _____

I am _____

I am _____

I am _____

I am _____

I am _____

I am _____

I am _____

I am _____

I am _____

I am _____

I am _____

I am _____

I am _____

I _____

I _____

I _____

I _____

I _____

"A little change is a big change if you do it right. #detailsmatter" - #LaGringa

Day 84: Today's Date: ___/___/____

I am _____

I am _____

I am _____

I am _____

I am _____

I am _____

I am _____

I am _____

I am _____

I am _____

I am _____

I am _____

I am _____

I am _____

I am _____

I _____

I _____

I _____

I _____

I _____

"Always hit first." - #LaGringa

Day 85: Today's Date: ___/___/____

I am _____

I am _____

I am _____

I am _____

I am _____

I am _____

I am _____

I am _____

I am _____

I am _____

I am _____

I am _____

I am _____

I am _____

I am _____

I _____

I _____

I _____

I _____

I _____

"In order to find your Queen or King you first need to be a Queen or King yourself."
- #LaGringa

Day 86: Today's Date: ___/___/____

I am _____

I am _____

I am _____

I am _____

I am _____

I am _____

I am _____

I am _____

I am _____

I am _____

I am _____

I am _____

I am _____

I am _____

I am _____

I am _____

I _____

I _____

I _____

I _____

I _____

"Sound the alarms, I'm bringing the fire!!!!!" - #LaGringa

Day 87: Today's Date: ___/___/____

I am _____

I am _____

I am _____

I am _____

I am _____

I am _____

I am _____

I am _____

I am _____

I am _____

I am _____

I am _____

I am _____

I am _____

I am _____

I am _____

I _____

I _____

I _____

I _____

I _____

"Tu eres increíble." - #LaGringa

Day 88: Today's Date: ___/___/____

I am _____

I am _____

I am _____

I am _____

I am _____

I am _____

I am _____

I am _____

I am _____

I am _____

I am _____

I am _____

I am _____

I am _____

I am _____

I _____

I _____

I _____

I _____

I _____

"Quiero experimentar todo en el mundo." - #LaGringa

Day 89: Today's Date: ___/___/____

I am _____

I am _____

I am _____

I am _____

I am _____

I am _____

I am _____

I am _____

I am _____

I am _____

I am _____

I am _____

I am _____

I am _____

I am _____

I _____

I _____

I _____

I _____

I _____

"There is a SUPERSTAR in you. Let your light shine on the World!" - #LaGringa

Day 90: Today's Date: ___/___/____

I am _____

I am _____

I am _____

I am _____

I am _____

I am _____

I am _____

I am _____

I am _____

I am _____

I am _____

I am _____

I am _____

I am _____

I am _____

I _____

I _____

I _____

I _____

I _____

CONGRATULATIONS!!!

WOOOOOOOO!!!!! GO YOU!!!

You've completed your FIRST FULL 90 days of committing to I am statements every morning! That's right, you are CHANGING YOUR LIFE! Take some time to reflect. Recognizing your growth and being intentional in your plans will help you to get the most out of this practice!

On Days 60 – 90…

Did you WRITE every day? _____

Did you RECITE every day? _____

Did you LIGHT the World on fire every day? _____

Which of these three steps could you improve most in? How will you implement that moving forward?

What has changed for you over the past 30 days? What progress have you made? (Tip: Compare your day 60/61/62 journal entries to you most recent)

What would you like to get out of the <u>NEXT</u> 30 days?

**Mastermind Tip: Live your life in 90 day runs!!! Always set goals for the next 90 days that align with your overall vision. Day 180 HERE YOU COME!!!! …
Let's still do 30 day check ins though OK? Deal!**

STOP and fill out this page BEFORE moving forward.
Has this practice been impactful for you in the last 90 days?
(circle one)

YES   No   YES   Maybe   YES

If you circled YES… LOOK AT YOU ROCKIN IT!!!! Now it is time to pay it forward. You found out about this book because SOMEONE shared it, and it is changing your life. On day 30 you shared this book with 5 more people – how did that go? Are their lives now being changed? Whether you see it right now or not I am confident you had a MAJOR impact in their life. Now YOU have the power to change MORE people's lives simply by sharing this book with them!!!! It is time to impact the WORLD, again.

Who are 5 people in your life that you think could benefit from this practice?
1. _____
2. _____
3. _____
4. _____
5. _____

What can you do to make sure that they get a new copy of this journal in the next 10 days?
Meet up for coffee and explain to them how much this has impacted you
Send them a link to purchase the book on Amazon
Post it on Social media and tag them
Send them a text message about how impactful it has been for you
Hand write a letter to them about the impact and send it in the mail
Purchase them a copy as a gift

If you circled Maybe…
Have you honestly committed EVERY morning for the last 30 days straight?
What is causing you to waiver in your feelings towards this daily practice?
What could YOU do to turn your answer into a YES?

If you circled No…
Have you honestly committed EVERY morning for the last 30 days straight?
What about the exercise is making you feel uncomfortable?
How could you turn it around and make it impact the NEXT 30 days of your life?

"Considérelo hecho!" - #LaGringa

Day 91: Today's Date: ___/___/____

I am _____

I am _____

I am _____

I am _____

I am _____

I am _____

I am _____

I am _____

I am _____

I am _____

I am _____

I am _____

I am _____

I am _____

I am _____

I _____

I _____

I _____

I _____

I _____

"This is not a dress rehearsal. This is the only chance you get, so GO FOR IT." - #LaGringa

Day 92: Today's Date: ___/___/____

I am _____

I am _____

I am _____

I am _____

I am _____

I am _____

I am _____

I am _____

I am _____

I am _____

I am _____

I am _____

I am _____

I am _____

I am _____

I _____

I _____

I _____

I _____

I _____

**"Everything that has ever been done, once wasn't done before.
#impossibleISpossible" - #LaGringa**

Day 93: Today's Date: ___/___/____

I am _____

I am _____

I am _____

I am _____

I am _____

I am _____

I am _____

I am _____

I am _____

I am _____

I am _____

I am _____

I am _____

I am _____

I am _____

I _____

I _____

I _____

I _____

I _____

"You are a beautiful day." - #LaGringa

Day 94: Today's Date: ___/___/____

I am _____

I am _____

I am _____

I am _____

I am _____

I am _____

I am _____

I am _____

I am _____

I am _____

I am _____

I am _____

I am _____

I am _____

I am _____

I _____

I _____

I _____

I _____

I _____

"What makes you stronger? Do more of THAT." - #LaGringa

Day 95: Today's Date: ___/___/____

I am _____

I am _____

I am _____

I am _____

I am _____

I am _____

I am _____

I am _____

I am _____

I am _____

I am _____

I am _____

I am _____

I am _____

I am _____

I _____

I _____

I _____

I _____

I _____

"What goal do you have that pursuing scares you the most?" - #LaGringa

Day 96: Today's Date: ___/___/____

I am _____

I am _____

I am _____

I am _____

I am _____

I am _____

I am _____

I am _____

I am _____

I am _____

I am _____

I am _____

I am _____

I am _____

I am _____

I _____

I _____

I _____

I _____

I _____

"Vivo rapido." - #LaGringa

Day 97: Today's Date: ___/___/____

I am _____

I am _____

I am _____

I am _____

I am _____

I am _____

I am _____

I am _____

I am _____

I am _____

I am _____

I am _____

I am _____

I am _____

I am _____

I _____

I _____

I _____

I _____

I _____

"Negativity gets you unfollowed." - #LaGringa

Day 98: Today's Date: ___/___/____

I am _____

I am _____

I am _____

I am _____

I am _____

I am _____

I am _____

I am _____

I am _____

I am _____

I am _____

I am _____

I am _____

I am _____

I am _____

I _____

I _____

I _____

I _____

I _____

"The World is FULL of abundance. GET YOURS." - #LaGringa

Day 99: Today's Date: ___/___/____

I am _____

I am _____

I am _____

I am _____

I am _____

I am _____

I am _____

I am _____

I am _____

I am _____

I am _____

I am _____

I am _____

I am _____

I am _____

I _____

I _____

I _____

I _____

I _____

"It's always happy hour if you're focused on the right things." - #LaGringa

Day 100: Today's Date: ___/___/____

I am _____

I am _____

I am _____

I am _____

I am _____

I am _____

I am _____

I am _____

I am _____

I am _____

I am _____

I am _____

I am _____

I am _____

I am _____

I _____

I _____

I _____

I _____

I _____

"Love is friendship on fire." - #LaGringa

Day 101: Today's Date: ___/___/____

I am _____

I am _____

I am _____

I am _____

I am _____

I am _____

I am _____

I am _____

I am _____

I am _____

I am _____

I am _____

I am _____

I am _____

I am _____

I _____

I _____

I _____

I _____

I _____

"What would happen to your life if you have no choice but to aggressively pursue your goals with MASSIVE action?" - #LaGringa

Day 102: Today's Date: ___/___/____

I am _____

I am _____

I am _____

I am _____

I am _____

I am _____

I am _____

I am _____

I am _____

I am _____

I am _____

I am _____

I am _____

I am _____

I am _____

I _____

I _____

I _____

I _____

I _____

"Eat, Sleep, Grind, Repeat." - #LaGringa

Day 103: Today's Date: ___/___/____

I am _____

I am _____

I am _____

I am _____

I am _____

I am _____

I am _____

I am _____

I am _____

I am _____

I am _____

I am _____

I am _____

I am _____

I am _____

I _____

I _____

I _____

I _____

I _____

"Siempre dara gran valor a los demas en su vida." - #LaGringa

Day 104: Today's Date: ___/___/____

I am _____

I am _____

I am _____

I am _____

I am _____

I am _____

I am _____

I am _____

I am _____

I am _____

I am _____

I am _____

I am _____

I am _____

I am _____

I _____

I _____

I _____

I _____

I _____

"Me encanta amor." - #LaGringa

Day 105: Today's Date: ___/___/____

I am _____

I am _____

I am _____

I am _____

I am _____

I am _____

I am _____

I am _____

I am _____

I am _____

I am _____

I am _____

I am _____

I am _____

I am _____

I _____

I _____

I _____

I _____

I _____

"You're not going to feel ready. Do it ANYWAYS." - #LaGringa

Day 106: Today's Date: ___/___/____

I am _____

I am _____

I am _____

I am _____

I am _____

I am _____

I am _____

I am _____

I am _____

I am _____

I am _____

I am _____

I am _____

I am _____

I am _____

I _____

I _____

I _____

I _____

I _____

"What would happen if you took the word maybe out of your vocabulary when making decisions?." - #LaGringa

Day 107: Today's Date: ___/___/___

I am _____

I am _____

I am _____

I am _____

I am _____

I am _____

I am _____

I am _____

I am _____

I am _____

I am _____

I am _____

I am _____

I am _____

I am _____

I _____

I _____

I _____

I _____

I _____

"Ganamos juntos!" - #LaGringa

Day 108: Today's Date: ___/___/____

I am _____

I am _____

I am _____

I am _____

I am _____

I am _____

I am _____

I am _____

I am _____

I am _____

I am _____

I am _____

I am _____

I am _____

I am _____

I _____

I _____

I _____

I _____

I _____

"Estoy vendecida." - #LaGringa

Day 109: Today's Date: ___/___/___

I am _____

I am _____

I am _____

I am _____

I am _____

I am _____

I am _____

I am _____

I am _____

I am _____

I am _____

I am _____

I am _____

I am _____

I am _____

I _____

I _____

I _____

I _____

I _____

"Don't let anyone tell you what's possible. Do the impossible." - #LaGringa

Day 110: Today's Date: ___/___/____

I am _____

I am _____

I am _____

I am _____

I am _____

I am _____

I am _____

I am _____

I am _____

I am _____

I am _____

I am _____

I am _____

I am _____

I am _____

I _____

I _____

I _____

I _____

I _____

"Day 111, that's like 11:11, so make a wish!!!" - #LaGringa

Day 111: Today's Date: ___/___/____

I am _____

I am _____

I am _____

I am _____

I am _____

I am _____

I am _____

I am _____

I am _____

I am _____

I am _____

I am _____

I am _____

I am _____

I am _____

I _____

I _____

I _____

I _____

I _____

"Pay attention to people who support you." - #LaGringa

Day 112: Today's Date: ___/___/____

I am _____

I am _____

I am _____

I am _____

I am _____

I am _____

I am _____

I am _____

I am _____

I am _____

I am _____

I am _____

I am _____

I am _____

I am _____

I _____

I _____

I _____

I _____

I _____

"En un jardin de un million de flores hermosas, tu eres la mas maravilosa." - #LaGringa

Day 113: Today's Date: ___/___/____

I am _____

I am _____

I am _____

I am _____

I am _____

I am _____

I am _____

I am _____

I am _____

I am _____

I am _____

I am _____

I am _____

I am _____

I am _____

I _____

I _____

I _____

I _____

I _____

"Be EXTRA, otherwise you're just ordinary." - #LaGringa

Day 114: Today's Date: ___/___/____

I am _____

I am _____

I am _____

I am _____

I am _____

I am _____

I am _____

I am _____

I am _____

I am _____

I am _____

I am _____

I am _____

I am _____

I am _____

I _____

I _____

I _____

I _____

I _____

"Make the phone call, cast the first line." - #LaGringa

Day 115: Today's Date: ___/___/____

I am _____

I am _____

I am _____

I am _____

I am _____

I am _____

I am _____

I am _____

I am _____

I am _____

I am _____

I am _____

I am _____

I am _____

I am _____

I _____

I _____

I _____

I _____

I _____

"YOU are an exciting thing to see." - #LaGringa

Day 116: Today's Date: ___/___/____

I am _____

I am _____

I am _____

I am _____

I am _____

I am _____

I am _____

I am _____

I am _____

I am _____

I am _____

I am _____

I am _____

I am _____

I am _____

I _____

I _____

I _____

I _____

I _____

"Create the universe you want in your mind." - #LaGringa

Day 117: Today's Date: ___/___/___

I am _____

I am _____

I am _____

I am _____

I am _____

I am _____

I am _____

I am _____

I am _____

I am _____

I am _____

I am _____

I am _____

I am _____

I _____

I _____

I _____

I _____

I _____

"Become the type of person you want to surround yourself with." - #LaGringa

Day 118: Today's Date: ___/___/____

I am _____

I am _____

I am _____

I am _____

I am _____

I am _____

I am _____

I am _____

I am _____

I am _____

I am _____

I am _____

I am _____

I am _____

I am _____

I _____

I _____

I _____

I _____

I _____

"If you make enough attempts you'll stumble on success, and then you'll start to get success on purpose. Taking the first action is the key." - #LaGringa

Day 119: Today's Date: ___/___/____

I am _____

I am _____

I am _____

I am _____

I am _____

I am _____

I am _____

I am _____

I am _____

I am _____

I am _____

I am _____

I am _____

I am _____

I am _____

I am _____

I _____

I _____

I _____

I _____

I _____

"The key to success is VOLUME." - #LaGringa

Day 120: Today's Date: ___/___/____

I am _____

I am _____

I am _____

I am _____

I am _____

I am _____

I am _____

I am _____

I am _____

I am _____

I am _____

I am _____

I am _____

I am _____

I am _____

I _____

I _____

I _____

I _____

I _____

CONGRATULATIONS!!!

YOU ARE FLIPPIN' KILLIN' IT!!!

You've completed your fourth 30 day run of committing to I am statements every morning! Every single day you are CHANGING YOUR LIFE! Take some time to reflect. Recognizing your growth and being intentional in your plans will help you to get the most out of this practice!

On Days 90 – 120 …

Did you WRITE every day? _____

Did you RECITE every day? _____

Did you LIGHT the World on fire every day? _____

Which of these three steps could you improve most in? How will you implement that moving forward?

What has changed for you over the past 30 days? What progress have you made? (Tip: Compare your day 90/91/92 journal entries to you most recent)

What would you like to get out of the <u>NEXT</u> 30 days?

See you in 30 days mi amigo!!!

"Create your own luck." - #LaGringa

Day 121: Today's Date: ___/___/____

I am _____

I am _____

I am _____

I am _____

I am _____

I am _____

I am _____

I am _____

I am _____

I am _____

I am _____

I am _____

I am _____

I am _____

I am _____

I _____

I _____

I _____

I _____

I _____

"The payoff of what you do today will be life changing tomorrow." - #LaGringa

Day 122: Today's Date: ___/___/____

I am _____

I am _____

I am _____

I am _____

I am _____

I am _____

I am _____

I am _____

I am _____

I am _____

I am _____

I am _____

I am _____

I am _____

I am _____

I _____

I _____

I _____

I _____

I _____

"The 1% understand the importance of volume. Don't take one action step, take thousands." - #LaGringa

Day 123: Today's Date: ___/___/____

I am _____

I am _____

I am _____

I am _____

I am _____

I am _____

I am _____

I am _____

I am _____

I am _____

I am _____

I am _____

I am _____

I am _____

I am _____

I _____

I _____

I _____

I _____

I _____

"Be persistent." - #LaGringa

Day 124: Today's Date: ___/___/____

I am _____

I am _____

I am _____

I am _____

I am _____

I am _____

I am _____

I am _____

I am _____

I am _____

I am _____

I am _____

I am _____

I am _____

I am _____

I _____

I _____

I _____

I _____

I _____

"Move in the opposite direction of what feels comfortable." - #LaGringa

Day 125: Today's Date: ___/___/____

I am _____

I am _____

I am _____

I am _____

I am _____

I am _____

I am _____

I am _____

I am _____

I am _____

I am _____

I am _____

I am _____

I am _____

I am _____

I _____

I _____

I _____

I _____

I _____

"The only way you can ever get there is by moving forward. One step, one jump, one leap at a time." - #LaGringa

Day 126: Today's Date: ___/___/___

I am _____

I am _____

I am _____

I am _____

I am _____

I am _____

I am _____

I am _____

I am _____

I am _____

I am _____

I am _____

I am _____

I am _____

I am _____

I _____

I _____

I _____

I _____

I _____

"Social media in an incredible tool to learn about someone because you see what they cared about 5 minutes ago." - #LaGringa

Day 127: Today's Date: ___/___/____

I am _____

I am _____

I am _____

I am _____

I am _____

I am _____

I am _____

I am _____

I am _____

I am _____

I am _____

I am _____

I am _____

I am _____

I am _____

I _____

I _____

I _____

I _____

I _____

"Learn something about someone new every day." - #LaGringa

Day 128: Today's Date: ___/___/___

I am _____

I am _____

I am _____

I am _____

I am _____

I am _____

I am _____

I am _____

I am _____

I am _____

I am _____

I am _____

I am _____

I am _____

I am _____

I _____

I _____

I _____

I _____

I _____

"Meet someone special today." - #LaGringa

Day 129: Today's Date: ___/___/____

I am _____

I am _____

I am _____

I am _____

I am _____

I am _____

I am _____

I am _____

I am _____

I am _____

I am _____

I am _____

I am _____

I am _____

I am _____

I _____

I _____

I _____

I _____

I _____

"Double down on the future." - #LaGringa

Day 130: Today's Date: ___/___/____

I am _____

I am _____

I am _____

I am _____

I am _____

I am _____

I am _____

I am _____

I am _____

I am _____

I am _____

I am _____

I am _____

I am _____

I am _____

I am _____

I _____

I _____

I _____

I _____

I _____

"Read a book cover to cover, TODAY." - #LaGringa

Day 131: Today's Date: ___/___/____

I am _____

I am _____

I am _____

I am _____

I am _____

I am _____

I am _____

I am _____

I am _____

I am _____

I am _____

I am _____

I am _____

I am _____

I am _____

I _____

I _____

I _____

I _____

I _____

"Do you realize that yesterday is already gone?" - #LaGringa

Day 132: Today's Date: ___/___/____

I am _____

I am _____

I am _____

I am _____

I am _____

I am _____

I am _____

I am _____

I am _____

I am _____

I am _____

I am _____

I am _____

I am _____

I am _____

I _____

I _____

I _____

I _____

I _____

"Don't look for easy, look for the grind, look for worth it." - #LaGringa

Day 133: Today's Date: ___/___/____

I am _____

I am _____

I am _____

I am _____

I am _____

I am _____

I am _____

I am _____

I am _____

I am _____

I am _____

I am _____

I am _____

I am _____

I am _____

I _____

I _____

I _____

I _____

I _____

"Be infinitely grateful for the abundance in your life." - #LaGringa

Day 134: Today's Date: ___/___/____

I am _____

I am _____

I am _____

I am _____

I am _____

I am _____

I am _____

I am _____

I am _____

I am _____

I am _____

I am _____

I am _____

I am _____

I am _____

I _____

I _____

I _____

I _____

I _____

"Tomorrow will come whether or not you're ready for it, and when it does it will be now." - #LaGringa

Day 135: Today's Date: ___/___/____

I am _____

I am _____

I am _____

I am _____

I am _____

I am _____

I am _____

I am _____

I am _____

I am _____

I am _____

I am _____

I am _____

I am _____

I am _____

I _____

I _____

I _____

I _____

I _____

"The rear view mirror is only useful if you want to back up." - #LaGringa

Day 136: Today's Date: ___/___/____

I am _____

I am _____

I am _____

I am _____

I am _____

I am _____

I am _____

I am _____

I am _____

I am _____

I am _____

I am _____

I am _____

I am _____

I am _____

I am _____

I _____

I _____

I _____

I _____

I _____

"What you do today will be evident in your life tomorrow." - #LaGringa

Day 137: Today's Date: ___/___/____

I am _____

I am _____

I am _____

I am _____

I am _____

I am _____

I am _____

I am _____

I am _____

I am _____

I am _____

I am _____

I am _____

I am _____

I am _____

I _____

I _____

I _____

I _____

I _____

"Tu sonrisa es marvilloso." - #LaGringa

Day 138: Today's Date: ___/___/____

I am _____

I am _____

I am _____

I am _____

I am _____

I am _____

I am _____

I am _____

I am _____

I am _____

I am _____

I am _____

I am _____

I am _____

I am _____

I _____

I _____

I _____

I _____

I _____

"The World is a beautiful place, take time to look around and appreciate it."
- #LaGringa

Day 139: Today's Date: ___/___/____

I am _____

I am _____

I am _____

I am _____

I am _____

I am _____

I am _____

I am _____

I am _____

I am _____

I am _____

I am _____

I am _____

I am _____

I am _____

I _____

I _____

I _____

I _____

I _____

"Today have breakfast with a view." - #LaGringa

Day 140: Today's Date: ___/___/____

I am _____

I am _____

I am _____

I am _____

I am _____

I am _____

I am _____

I am _____

I am _____

I am _____

I am _____

I am _____

I am _____

I am _____

I am _____

I _____

I _____

I _____

I _____

I _____

"When other people are out reporting on pop-culture, be out there CREATING pop-culture." - #LaGringa

Day 141: Today's Date: ___/___/____

I am _____

I am _____

I am _____

I am _____

I am _____

I am _____

I am _____

I am _____

I am _____

I am _____

I am _____

I am _____

I am _____

I am _____

I am _____

I _____

I _____

I _____

I _____

I _____

"Be a player not a spectator." - #LaGringa

Day 142: Today's Date: ___/___/____

I am _____

I am _____

I am _____

I am _____

I am _____

I am _____

I am _____

I am _____

I am _____

I am _____

I am _____

I am _____

I am _____

I am _____

I am _____

I _____

I _____

I _____

I _____

I _____

"Engage in experiences." - #LaGringa

Day 143: Today's Date: ___/___/____

I am _____

I am _____

I am _____

I am _____

I am _____

I am _____

I am _____

I am _____

I am _____

I am _____

I am _____

I am _____

I am _____

I am _____

I am _____

I _____

I _____

I _____

I _____

I _____

"Just know that you are never alone." - #LaGringa

Day 144: Today's Date: ___/___/___

I am _____

I am _____

I am _____

I am _____

I am _____

I am _____

I am _____

I am _____

I am _____

I am _____

I am _____

I am _____

I am _____

I am _____

I am _____

I _____

I _____

I _____

I _____

I _____

"I am impressed with you today." - #LaGringa

Day 145: Today's Date: ___/___/___

I am _____

I am _____

I am _____

I am _____

I am _____

I am _____

I am _____

I am _____

I am _____

I am _____

I am _____

I am _____

I am _____

I am _____

I am _____

I _____

I _____

I _____

I _____

I _____

"Get people addicted to you, start NOW." - #LaGringa

Day 146: Today's Date: ___/___/____

I am _____

I am _____

I am _____

I am _____

I am _____

I am _____

I am _____

I am _____

I am _____

I am _____

I am _____

I am _____

I am _____

I am _____

I am _____

I _____

I _____

I _____

I _____

I _____

"When life says yes, say thank you." - #LaGringa

Day 147: Today's Date: ___/___/____

I am _____

I am _____

I am _____

I am _____

I am _____

I am _____

I am _____

I am _____

I am _____

I am _____

I am _____

I am _____

I am _____

I am _____

I am _____

I _____

I _____

I _____

I _____

I _____

"When you go somewhere, bring someone back a gift." - #LaGringa

Day 148: Today's Date: ___/___/____

I am _____

I am _____

I am _____

I am _____

I am _____

I am _____

I am _____

I am _____

I am _____

I am _____

I am _____

I am _____

I am _____

I am _____

I am _____

I _____

I _____

I _____

I _____

I _____

"Happiness, Wealth, Abundance. Health. It can all be yours if you choose it to be."
- #LaGringa

Day 149: Today's Date: ___/___/____

I am _____

I am _____

I am _____

I am _____

I am _____

I am _____

I am _____

I am _____

I am _____

I am _____

I am _____

I am _____

I am _____

I am _____

I am _____

I am _____

I _____

I _____

I _____

I _____

I _____

"Make YOURSELF a celebrity by letting people into your life." - #LaGringa

Day 150: Today's Date: ___/___/____

I am _____

I am _____

I am _____

I am _____

I am _____

I am _____

I am _____

I am _____

I am _____

I am _____

I am _____

I am _____

I am _____

I am _____

I am _____

I _____

I _____

I _____

I _____

I _____

CONGRATULATIONS!!!

QUE INCREIBLE!!!!

You've completed a 30 day run of committing to I am statements every morning for the FITH TIME! It must feel pretty natural by now!!! Every single day you are CHANGING YOUR LIFE! Take some time to reflect. Recognizing your growth and being intentional in your plans will help you to get the most out of this practice!

On Days 120 - 150 …

Did you WRITE every day? _____

Did you RECITE every day? _____

Did you LIGHT the World on fire every day? _____

Which of these three steps could you improve most in? How will you implement that moving forward?

What has changed for you over the past 30 days? What progress have you made? (Tip: Compare your day 120/121/122 journal entries to you most recent)

What would you like to get out of the <u>NEXT</u> 30 days?

Lets commit now to another 30 AMAZING days together!!! READY… Set… GO!!!!!!!!!!

"Stop trying to do it alone. There is help, accept it. Build a team." - #LaGringa

Day 151: Today's Date: ___/___/____

I am _____

I am _____

I am _____

I am _____

I am _____

I am _____

I am _____

I am _____

I am _____

I am _____

I am _____

I am _____

I am _____

I am _____

I am _____

I _____

I _____

I _____

I _____

I _____

"Who could help you on your journey today? Have you told them? Do they know what you need them to do?" - #LaGringa

Day 152: Today's Date: ___/___/____

I am _____

I am _____

I am _____

I am _____

I am _____

I am _____

I am _____

I am _____

I am _____

I am _____

I am _____

I am _____

I am _____

I am _____

I am _____

I _____

I _____

I _____

I _____

I _____

"People can't read your mind, tell them what you think." - #LaGringa

Day 153: Today's Date: ___/___/____

I am _____

I am _____

I am _____

I am _____

I am _____

I am _____

I am _____

I am _____

I am _____

I am _____

I am _____

I am _____

I am _____

I am _____

I am _____

I _____

I _____

I _____

I _____

I _____

"Know your self-worth. Have self-respect. You deserve it." - #LaGringa

Day 154: Today's Date: ___/___/____

I am _____

I am _____

I am _____

I am _____

I am _____

I am _____

I am _____

I am _____

I am _____

I am _____

I am _____

I am _____

I am _____

I am _____

I am _____

I _____

I _____

I _____

I _____

I _____

"It is your responsibility, and no one else's, to put yourself first." - #LaGringa

Day 155: Today's Date: ___/___/____

I am _____

I am _____

I am _____

I am _____

I am _____

I am _____

I am _____

I am _____

I am _____

I am _____

I am _____

I am _____

I am _____

I am _____

I am _____

I _____

I _____

I _____

I _____

I _____

"Only you know what is best for you." - #LaGringa

Day 156: Today's Date: ___/___/____

I am _____

I am _____

I am _____

I am _____

I am _____

I am _____

I am _____

I am _____

I am _____

I am _____

I am _____

I am _____

I am _____

I am _____

I am _____

I _____

I _____

I _____

I _____

I _____

"Send out good vibes to the World today." - #LaGringa

Day 157: Today's Date: ___/___/____

I am _____

I am _____

I am _____

I am _____

I am _____

I am _____

I am _____

I am _____

I am _____

I am _____

I am _____

I am _____

I am _____

I am _____

I am _____

I _____

I _____

I _____

I _____

I _____

"If you were an instrument, what would your song sound like?" - #LaGringa

Day 158: Today's Date: ___/___/____

I am _____

I am _____

I am _____

I am _____

I am _____

I am _____

I am _____

I am _____

I am _____

I am _____

I am _____

I am _____

I am _____

I am _____

I am _____

I _____

I _____

I _____

I _____

I _____

"Build a library." - #LaGringa

Day 159: Today's Date: ___/___/____

I am _____

I am _____

I am _____

I am _____

I am _____

I am _____

I am _____

I am _____

I am _____

I am _____

I am _____

I am _____

I am _____

I am _____

I am _____

I _____

I _____

I _____

I _____

I _____

"Only you can live for you." - #LaGringa

Day 160: Today's Date: ___/___/____

I am _____

I am _____

I am _____

I am _____

I am _____

I am _____

I am _____

I am _____

I am _____

I am _____

I am _____

I am _____

I am _____

I am _____

I am _____

I _____

I _____

I _____

I _____

I _____

"Now is the only time that ever exists." - #LaGringa

Day 161: Today's Date: ___/___/____

I am _____

I am _____

I am _____

I am _____

I am _____

I am _____

I am _____

I am _____

I am _____

I am _____

I am _____

I am _____

I am _____

I am _____

I am _____

I _____

I _____

I _____

I _____

I _____

"Give yourself a future birthday present." - #LaGringa

Day 162: Today's Date: ___/___/____

I am _____

I am _____

I am _____

I am _____

I am _____

I am _____

I am _____

I am _____

I am _____

I am _____

I am _____

I am _____

I am _____

I am _____

I am _____

I _____

I _____

I _____

I _____

I _____

"Always be at home." - #LaGringa

Day 163: Today's Date: ___/___/____

I am _____

I am _____

I am _____

I am _____

I am _____

I am _____

I am _____

I am _____

I am _____

I am _____

I am _____

I am _____

I am _____

I am _____

I am _____

I _____

I _____

I _____

I _____

I _____

"Never stay inside." - #LaGringa

Day 164: Today's Date: ___/___/____

I am _____

I am _____

I am _____

I am _____

I am _____

I am _____

I am _____

I am _____

I am _____

I am _____

I am _____

I am _____

I am _____

I am _____

I am _____

I _____

I _____

I _____

I _____

I _____

"Plant a garden of plants that you want to see grow." - #LaGringa

Day 165: Today's Date: ___/___/____

I am _____

I am _____

I am _____

I am _____

I am _____

I am _____

I am _____

I am _____

I am _____

I am _____

I am _____

I am _____

I am _____

I am _____

I am _____

I _____

I _____

I _____

I _____

I _____

"Everything you want, need, and seek is already inside of you." - #LaGringa

Day 166: Today's Date: ___/___/____

I am _____

I am _____

I am _____

I am _____

I am _____

I am _____

I am _____

I am _____

I am _____

I am _____

I am _____

I am _____

I am _____

I am _____

I am _____

I _____

I _____

I _____

I _____

I _____

"Abundance is a mindset." - #LaGringa

Day 167: Today's Date: ___/___/____

I am _____

I am _____

I am _____

I am _____

I am _____

I am _____

I am _____

I am _____

I am _____

I am _____

I am _____

I am _____

I am _____

I am _____

I am _____

I _____

I _____

I _____

I _____

I _____

**"I wonder what I'll think about this book and these quotes 5 years from now...
Hi future Janine!!!" - #LaGringa**

Day 168: Today's Date: ___/___/____

I am _____

I am _____

I am _____

I am _____

I am _____

I am _____

I am _____

I am _____

I am _____

I am _____

I am _____

I am _____

I am _____

I am _____

I am _____

I _____

I _____

I _____

I _____

I _____

"Be here to serve. How can you make someone else's day better today?" - #LaGringa

Day 169: Today's Date: ___/___/___

I am _____

I am _____

I am _____

I am _____

I am _____

I am _____

I am _____

I am _____

I am _____

I am _____

I am _____

I am _____

I am _____

I am _____

I am _____

I _____

I _____

I _____

I _____

I _____

"The most essential ingredient to your success is YOU." - #LaGringa

Day 170: Today's Date: ___/___/____

I am _____

I am _____

I am _____

I am _____

I am _____

I am _____

I am _____

I am _____

I am _____

I am _____

I am _____

I am _____

I am _____

I am _____

I am _____

I _____

I _____

I _____

I _____

I _____

"Love yourself like you would love a puppy." - #LaGringa

Day 171: Today's Date: ___/___/____

I am _____

I am _____

I am _____

I am _____

I am _____

I am _____

I am _____

I am _____

I am _____

I am _____

I am _____

I am _____

I am _____

I am _____

I am _____

I _____

I _____

I _____

I _____

I _____

"Do you feed your mind, drown it, or starve it?" - #LaGringa

Day 172: Today's Date: ___/___/____

I am _____

I am _____

I am _____

I am _____

I am _____

I am _____

I am _____

I am _____

I am _____

I am _____

I am _____

I am _____

I am _____

I am _____

I am _____

I _____

I _____

I _____

I _____

I _____

"You have something to say that someone else needs to hear. Say it." - #LaGringa

Day 173: Today's Date: ___/___/___

I am _____

I am _____

I am _____

I am _____

I am _____

I am _____

I am _____

I am _____

I am _____

I am _____

I am _____

I am _____

I am _____

I am _____

I am _____

I _____

I _____

I _____

I _____

I _____

"Fear is only in your mind." - #LaGringa

Day 174: Today's Date: ___/___/____

I am _____

I am _____

I am _____

I am _____

I am _____

I am _____

I am _____

I am _____

I am _____

I am _____

I am _____

I am _____

I am _____

I am _____

I am _____

I _____

I _____

I _____

I _____

I _____

"Jealousy is a great indication of a goal you are afraid to have." - #LaGringa

Day 175: Today's Date: ___/___/____

I am _____

I am _____

I am _____

I am _____

I am _____

I am _____

I am _____

I am _____

I am _____

I am _____

I am _____

I am _____

I am _____

I am _____

I am _____

I _____

I _____

I _____

I _____

I _____

"Mind muscle connection. Stay present." - #LaGringa

Day 176: Today's Date: ___/___/____

I am _____

I am _____

I am _____

I am _____

I am _____

I am _____

I am _____

I am _____

I am _____

I am _____

I am _____

I am _____

I am _____

I am _____

I am _____

I _____

I _____

I _____

I _____

I _____

"Know that you can, and you can. Decide that you will, and you will." - #LaGringa

Day 177: Today's Date: ___/___/___

I am _____

I am _____

I am _____

I am _____

I am _____

I am _____

I am _____

I am _____

I am _____

I am _____

I am _____

I am _____

I am _____

I am _____

I am _____

I _____

I _____

I _____

I _____

I _____

"Your authentic intention and solid commitment will bring into life whatever you choose." - #LaGringa

Day 178: Today's Date: ___/___/____

I am _____

I am _____

I am _____

I am _____

I am _____

I am _____

I am _____

I am _____

I am _____

I am _____

I am _____

I am _____

I am _____

I am _____

I am _____

I _____

I _____

I _____

I _____

I _____

"Know you can, go make it happen, and what you truly desire you will most certainly achieve." - #LaGringa

Day 179: Today's Date: ___/___/____

I am _____

I am _____

I am _____

I am _____

I am _____

I am _____

I am _____

I am _____

I am _____

I am _____

I am _____

I am _____

I am _____

I am _____

I am _____

I _____

I _____

I _____

I _____

I _____

"Just because an achievement is not easy or instantaneous, doesn't mean it's impossible or out of your reach." - #LaGringa

Day 180: Today's Date: ___/___/____

I am _____

I am _____

I am _____

I am _____

I am _____

I am _____

I am _____

I am _____

I am _____

I am _____

I am _____

I am _____

I am _____

I am _____

I am _____

I _____

I _____

I _____

I _____

I _____

CONGRATULATIONS!!!

JOURNAL GAME STRONG!

You've completed a SIX, count them 1…2..3..4..5….6!!!! 30 day runs of committing to I am statements every morning! THAT IS TWO FULL 90 DAY RUNS!!!! You are basically a journaling ROCK STAR!!! Every single day you are CHANGING YOUR LIFE! Take some time to reflect. Recognizing your growth and being intentional in your plans will help you to get the most out of this practice!

On Days 150 – 180…

Did you WRITE every day? _____

Did you RECITE every day? _____

Did you LIGHT the World on fire every day? _____

Which of these three steps could you improve most in? How will you implement that moving forward?

Lets look WAY back this time… What has changed for you over the past 180 days? What progress have you made? (Tip: Compare your day 1/2/3 journal entries to you most recent)

What would you like to get out of the <u>NEXT</u> 30 days?

Time to commit now to another 90 DAY RUN with 30 day challenges and check ins!!!!!!!

STOP and fill out this page BEFORE moving forward.
Has this practice been impactful for you in the last 90 days?
(circle one)

YES   No   YES   Maybe   YES

If you circled YES… LOOK AT YOU ROCKIN IT!!!! Now it is time to pay it forward. You found out about this book because SOMEONE shared it, and it is changing your life. On day 90 you shared this book with 5 more people – how did that go? Are their lives now being changed? Whether you see it right now or not I am confident you had a MAJOR impact in their life. Now YOU have the power to change MORE people's lives simply by sharing this book with them!!!! It is time to impact the WORLD, again.

Who are 5 people in your life that you think could benefit from this practice?
1. _____
2. _____
3. _____
4. _____
5. _____

What can you do to make sure that they get a new copy of this journal in the next 10 days?
Meet up for coffee and explain to them how much this has impacted you
Send them a link to purchase the book on Amazon
Post it on Social media and tag them
Send them a text message about how impactful it has been for you
Hand write a letter to them about the impact and send it in the mail
Purchase them a copy as a gift

If you circled Maybe…
Have you honestly committed EVERY morning for the last 30 days straight?
What is causing you to waiver in your feelings towards this daily practice?
What could YOU do to turn your answer into a YES?

If you circled No…
Have you honestly committed EVERY morning for the last 30 days straight?
What about the exercise is making you feel uncomfortable?
How could you turn it around and make it impact the NEXT 30 days of your life?

"Guess what? I believe in you!" - #LaGringa

Day 181: Today's Date: ___/___/____

I am _____

I am _____

I am _____

I am _____

I am _____

I am _____

I am _____

I am _____

I am _____

I am _____

I am _____

I am _____

I am _____

I am _____

I am _____

I _____

I _____

I _____

I _____

I _____

"Live your PASSION." - #LaGringa

Day 182: Today's Date: ___/___/____

I am _____

I am _____

I am _____

I am _____

I am _____

I am _____

I am _____

I am _____

I am _____

I am _____

I am _____

I am _____

I am _____

I am _____

I am _____

I _____

I _____

I _____

I _____

I _____

"If you don't change the World will change without you." - #LaGringa

Day 183: Today's Date: ___/___/____

I am _____

I am _____

I am _____

I am _____

I am _____

I am _____

I am _____

I am _____

I am _____

I am _____

I am _____

I am _____

I am _____

I am _____

I am _____

I _____

I _____

I _____

I _____

I _____

"You can be whatever you think you can't if you just decide that you can."
- #LaGringa

Day 184: Today's Date: ___/___/____

I am _____

I am _____

I am _____

I am _____

I am _____

I am _____

I am _____

I am _____

I am _____

I am _____

I am _____

I am _____

I am _____

I am _____

I am _____

I _____

I _____

I _____

I _____

I _____

"Everything I do, I do it MASSIVE." - #LaGringa

Day 185: Today's Date: ___/___/___

I am _____

I am _____

I am _____

I am _____

I am _____

I am _____

I am _____

I am _____

I am _____

I am _____

I am _____

I am _____

I am _____

I am _____

I am _____

I am _____

I _____

I _____

I _____

I _____

I _____

"Be HOTT." - #LaGringa

Day 186: Today's Date: ___/___/____

I am _____

I am _____

I am _____

I am _____

I am _____

I am _____

I am _____

I am _____

I am _____

I am _____

I am _____

I am _____

I am _____

I am _____

I am _____

I _____

I _____

I _____

I _____

I _____

"You are sexy." - #LaGringa

Day 187: Today's Date: ___/___/____

I am _____

I am _____

I am _____

I am _____

I am _____

I am _____

I am _____

I am _____

I am _____

I am _____

I am _____

I am _____

I am _____

I am _____

I am _____

I _____

I _____

I _____

I _____

I _____

"Look in the mirror, DAYYYMMNN you're PHENOMENAL!" - #LaGringa

Day 188: Today's Date: ___/___/____

I am _____

I am _____

I am _____

I am _____

I am _____

I am _____

I am _____

I am _____

I am _____

I am _____

I am _____

I am _____

I am _____

I am _____

I am _____

I _____

I _____

I _____

I _____

I _____

"Don't put up with bullshit, have standards." - #LaGringa

Day 189: Today's Date: ___/___/____

I am _____

I am _____

I am _____

I am _____

I am _____

I am _____

I am _____

I am _____

I am _____

I am _____

I am _____

I am _____

I am _____

I am _____

I am _____

I _____

I _____

I _____

I _____

I _____

"What if... money could buy happiness?" - #LaGringa

Day 190: Today's Date: ___/___/____

I am _____

I am _____

I am _____

I am _____

I am _____

I am _____

I am _____

I am _____

I am _____

I am _____

I am _____

I am _____

I am _____

I am _____

I am _____

I _____

I _____

I _____

I _____

I _____

"Do nothing but go after your goals." - #LaGringa

Day 191: Today's Date: ___/___/___

I am _____

I am _____

I am _____

I am _____

I am _____

I am _____

I am _____

I am _____

I am _____

I am _____

I am _____

I am _____

I am _____

I am _____

I am _____

I am _____

I _____

I _____

I _____

I _____

I _____

"Respect yourself. Respect others. Yourself comes FIRST." - #LaGringa

Day 192: Today's Date: ___/___/____

I am _____

I am _____

I am _____

I am _____

I am _____

I am _____

I am _____

I am _____

I am _____

I am _____

I am _____

I am _____

I am _____

I am _____

I am _____

I _____

I _____

I _____

I _____

I _____

"Spit fire DAILY." - #LaGringa

Day 193: Today's Date: ___/___/____

I am _____

I am _____

I am _____

I am _____

I am _____

I am _____

I am _____

I am _____

I am _____

I am _____

I am _____

I am _____

I am _____

I am _____

I am _____

I am _____

I _____

I _____

I _____

I _____

I _____

"Be better than you think you can." - #LaGringa

Day 194: Today's Date: ___/___/____

I am _____

I am _____

I am _____

I am _____

I am _____

I am _____

I am _____

I am _____

I am _____

I am _____

I am _____

I am _____

I am _____

I am _____

I am _____

I _____

I _____

I _____

I _____

I _____

"Someone in your same position or worse is going to get the life you want, so why not you?" - #LaGringa

Day 195: Today's Date: ___/___/____

I am _____

I am _____

I am _____

I am _____

I am _____

I am _____

I am _____

I am _____

I am _____

I am _____

I am _____

I am _____

I am _____

I am _____

I am _____

I _____

I _____

I _____

I _____

I _____

"You can have what you want." - #LaGringa

Day 196: Today's Date: ___/___/____

I am _____

I am _____

I am _____

I am _____

I am _____

I am _____

I am _____

I am _____

I am _____

I am _____

I am _____

I am _____

I am _____

I am _____

I am _____

I _____

I _____

I _____

I _____

I _____

"BE the person you are jealous of." - #LaGringa

Day 197: Today's Date: ___/___/____

I am _____

I am _____

I am _____

I am _____

I am _____

I am _____

I am _____

I am _____

I am _____

I am _____

I am _____

I am _____

I am _____

I am _____

I am _____

I _____

I _____

I _____

I _____

I _____

"Break through the boundaries you set for yourself." - #LaGringa

Day 198: Today's Date: ___/___/____

I am _____

I am _____

I am _____

I am _____

I am _____

I am _____

I am _____

I am _____

I am _____

I am _____

I am _____

I am _____

I am _____

I am _____

I am _____

I _____

I _____

I _____

I _____

I _____

"Carry yourself with confidence. Even if you aren't confident yet." - #LaGringa

Day 199: Today's Date: ___/___/____

I am _____

I am _____

I am _____

I am _____

I am _____

I am _____

I am _____

I am _____

I am _____

I am _____

I am _____

I am _____

I am _____

I am _____

I am _____

I _____

I _____

I _____

I _____

I _____

"Decide to be what you want. Right now." - #LaGringa

Day 200: Today's Date: ___/___/____

I am _____

I am _____

I am _____

I am _____

I am _____

I am _____

I am _____

I am _____

I am _____

I am _____

I am _____

I am _____

I am _____

I am _____

I am _____

I _____

I _____

I _____

I _____

I _____

"What if you wrote a book in 30 days?" - #LaGringa

Day 201: Today's Date: ___/___/____

I am _____

I am _____

I am _____

I am _____

I am _____

I am _____

I am _____

I am _____

I am _____

I am _____

I am _____

I am _____

I am _____

I am _____

I am _____

I _____

I _____

I _____

I _____

I _____

"There is no difference between you and the people who have achieved the success that you want." - #LaGringa

Day 202: Today's Date: ___/___/____

I am _____

I am _____

I am _____

I am _____

I am _____

I am _____

I am _____

I am _____

I am _____

I am _____

I am _____

I am _____

I am _____

I am _____

I am _____

I _____

I _____

I _____

I _____

I _____

"Join the people you want. Sit at the lunch table." - #LaGringa

Day 203: Today's Date: ___/___/____

I am _____

I am _____

I am _____

I am _____

I am _____

I am _____

I am _____

I am _____

I am _____

I am _____

I am _____

I am _____

I am _____

I am _____

I am _____

I _____

I _____

I _____

I _____

I _____

"YOU can do it. Go do it TODAY." - #LaGringa

Day 204: Today's Date: ___/___/____

I am _____

I am _____

I am _____

I am _____

I am _____

I am _____

I am _____

I am _____

I am _____

I am _____

I am _____

I am _____

I am _____

I am _____

I am _____

I _____

I _____

I _____

I _____

I _____

"Why? Because you can." - #LaGringa

Day 205: Today's Date: ___/___/____

I am _____

I am _____

I am _____

I am _____

I am _____

I am _____

I am _____

I am _____

I am _____

I am _____

I am _____

I am _____

I am _____

I am _____

I am _____

I am _____

I _____

I _____

I _____

I _____

I _____

"Tell someone a secret." - #LaGringa

Day 206: Today's Date: ___/___/____

I am _____

I am _____

I am _____

I am _____

I am _____

I am _____

I am _____

I am _____

I am _____

I am _____

I am _____

I am _____

I am _____

I am _____

I am _____

I _____

I _____

I _____

I _____

I _____

"If you graded yourself right now would you get an A+?" - #LaGringa

Day 207: Today's Date: ___/___/____

I am _____

I am _____

I am _____

I am _____

I am _____

I am _____

I am _____

I am _____

I am _____

I am _____

I am _____

I am _____

I am _____

I am _____

I am _____

I _____

I _____

I _____

I _____

I _____

"Create positive chatter." - #LaGringa

Day 208: Today's Date: ___/___/____

I am _____

I am _____

I am _____

I am _____

I am _____

I am _____

I am _____

I am _____

I am _____

I am _____

I am _____

I am _____

I am _____

I am _____

I am _____

I _____

I _____

I _____

I _____

I _____

"Be interested in other people's passions." - #LaGringa

Day 209: Today's Date: ___/___/____

I am _____

I am _____

I am _____

I am _____

I am _____

I am _____

I am _____

I am _____

I am _____

I am _____

I am _____

I am _____

I am _____

I am _____

I am _____

I _____

I _____

I _____

I _____

I _____

"Be all up on someone else's business. Fan their fire. Be positive." - #LaGringa

Day 210: Today's Date: ___/___/____

I am _____

I am _____

I am _____

I am _____

I am _____

I am _____

I am _____

I am _____

I am _____

I am _____

I am _____

I am _____

I am _____

I am _____

I am _____

I _____

I _____

I _____

I _____

I _____

CONGRATULATIONS!!!

YOU'RE DOING THE DANG THANG!!!

You've completed 30 day runs of committing to I am statements every morning 7 times in a ROW! Lucky number 7 baby!!!! I am so proud of you, and you should be extraordinarily proud of yourself. You may not feel it to the full extent but you CHANGING YOUR LIFE! Take some time to reflect. Recognizing your growth and being intentional in your plans will help you to get the most out of this practice!

On Days 180 – 210 …

Did you WRITE every day? _____

Did you RECITE every day? _____

Did you LIGHT the World on fire every day? _____

Which of these three steps could you improve most in? How will you implement that moving forward?

What has changed for you over the past 30 days? What progress have you made? (Tip: Compare your day 180/181/182 journal entries to you most recent)

What would you like to get out of the <u>NEXT</u> 30 days?

You're 1/3 of the day through your THIRD 90 DAY RUN – Keep that hustle muscle strong!

"Do for others what you want others to do for you." - #LaGringa

Day 211: Today's Date: ___/___/____

I am _____

I am _____

I am _____

I am _____

I am _____

I am _____

I am _____

I am _____

I am _____

I am _____

I am _____

I am _____

I am _____

I am _____

I am _____

I _____

I _____

I _____

I _____

I _____

"What was the last inspired thought you had?" - #LaGringa

Day 212: Today's Date: ___/___/____

I am _____

I am _____

I am _____

I am _____

I am _____

I am _____

I am _____

I am _____

I am _____

I am _____

I am _____

I am _____

I am _____

I am _____

I am _____

I _____

I _____

I _____

I _____

I _____

"People like people who like them." - #LaGringa

Day 213: Today's Date: ___/___/____

I am _____

I am _____

I am _____

I am _____

I am _____

I am _____

I am _____

I am _____

I am _____

I am _____

I am _____

I am _____

I am _____

I am _____

I am _____

I _____

I _____

I _____

I _____

I _____

"When you give people love, they give it back to you." - #LaGringa

Day 214: Today's Date: ___/___/___

I am _____

I am _____

I am _____

I am _____

I am _____

I am _____

I am _____

I am _____

I am _____

I am _____

I am _____

I am _____

I am _____

I am _____

I am _____

I _____

I _____

I _____

I _____

I _____

"Share good content." - #LaGringa

Day 215: Today's Date: ___/___/____

I am _____

I am _____

I am _____

I am _____

I am _____

I am _____

I am _____

I am _____

I am _____

I am _____

I am _____

I am _____

I am _____

I am _____

I am _____

I _____

I _____

I _____

I _____

I _____

"Be someone else's first follower." - #LaGringa

Day 216: Today's Date: ___/___/____

I am _____

I am _____

I am _____

I am _____

I am _____

I am _____

I am _____

I am _____

I am _____

I am _____

I am _____

I am _____

I am _____

I am _____

I am _____

I _____

I _____

I _____

I _____

I _____

"Don't be your own prisoner." - #LaGringa

Day 217: Today's Date: ___/___/____

I am _____

I am _____

I am _____

I am _____

I am _____

I am _____

I am _____

I am _____

I am _____

I am _____

I am _____

I am _____

I am _____

I am _____

I am _____

I _____

I _____

I _____

I _____

I _____

"It's not society that is stopping you, it's your perception of society." - #LaGringa

Day 218: Today's Date: ___/___/____

I am _____

I am _____

I am _____

I am _____

I am _____

I am _____

I am _____

I am _____

I am _____

I am _____

I am _____

I am _____

I am _____

I am _____

I am _____

I _____

I _____

I _____

I _____

I _____

"What if… what you thought they were thinking was the opposite of the what they were actually thinking?" - #LaGringa

Day 219: Today's Date: ___/___/____

I am _____

I am _____

I am _____

I am _____

I am _____

I am _____

I am _____

I am _____

I am _____

I am _____

I am _____

I am _____

I am _____

I am _____

I am _____

I _____

I _____

I _____

I _____

I _____

"Be active. Get out there." - #LaGringa

Day 220: Today's Date: ___/___/____

I am _____

I am _____

I am _____

I am _____

I am _____

I am _____

I am _____

I am _____

I am _____

I am _____

I am _____

I am _____

I am _____

I am _____

I am _____

I _____

I _____

I _____

I _____

I _____

"Make sure you're involved in life every day." - #LaGringa

Day 221: Today's Date: ___/___/____

I am _____

I am _____

I am _____

I am _____

I am _____

I am _____

I am _____

I am _____

I am _____

I am _____

I am _____

I am _____

I am _____

I am _____

I am _____

I _____

I _____

I _____

I _____

I _____

"Make yourself known." - #LaGringa

Day 222: Today's Date: ___/___/___

I am _____

I am _____

I am _____

I am _____

I am _____

I am _____

I am _____

I am _____

I am _____

I am _____

I am _____

I am _____

I am _____

I am _____

I am _____

I _____

I _____

I _____

I _____

I _____

"What if the person you're ignoring is your next best friend or next big customer?"
- #LaGringa

Day 223: Today's Date: ___/___/____

I am _____

I am _____

I am _____

I am _____

I am _____

I am _____

I am _____

I am _____

I am _____

I am _____

I am _____

I am _____

I am _____

I am _____

I am _____

I _____

I _____

I _____

I _____

I _____

"Use me." - #LaGringa

Day 224: Today's Date: ___/___/___

I am _____

I am _____

I am _____

I am _____

I am _____

I am _____

I am _____

I am _____

I am _____

I am _____

I am _____

I am _____

I am _____

I am _____

I am _____

I _____

I _____

I _____

I _____

I _____

"Shout out the people who make you feel good." - #LaGringa

Day 225: Today's Date: ___/___/____

I am _____

I am _____

I am _____

I am _____

I am _____

I am _____

I am _____

I am _____

I am _____

I am _____

I am _____

I am _____

I am _____

I am _____

I am _____

I _____

I _____

I _____

I _____

I _____

"You can start a following by being active." - #LaGringa

Day 226: Today's Date: ___/___/____

I am _____

I am _____

I am _____

I am _____

I am _____

I am _____

I am _____

I am _____

I am _____

I am _____

I am _____

I am _____

I am _____

I am _____

I am _____

I _____

I _____

I _____

I _____

I _____

"The only problem in your life is you." - #LaGringa

Day 227: Today's Date: ___/___/____

I am _____

I am _____

I am _____

I am _____

I am _____

I am _____

I am _____

I am _____

I am _____

I am _____

I am _____

I am _____

I am _____

I am _____

I am _____

I _____

I _____

I _____

I _____

I _____

"LOVE being EXTRA." - #LaGringa

Day 228: Today's Date: ___/___/____

I am _____

I am _____

I am _____

I am _____

I am _____

I am _____

I am _____

I am _____

I am _____

I am _____

I am _____

I am _____

I am _____

I am _____

I am _____

I _____

I _____

I _____

I _____

I _____

"Estoy aqui ahora." - #LaGringa

Day 229: Today's Date: ___/___/____

I am _____

I am _____

I am _____

I am _____

I am _____

I am _____

I am _____

I am _____

I am _____

I am _____

I am _____

I am _____

I am _____

I am _____

I am _____

I _____

I _____

I _____

I _____

I _____

"Start a tribe." - #LaGringa

Day 230: Today's Date: ___/___/____

I am _____

I am _____

I am _____

I am _____

I am _____

I am _____

I am _____

I am _____

I am _____

I am _____

I am _____

I am _____

I am _____

I am _____

I am _____

I am _____

I _____

I _____

I _____

I _____

I _____

"Don't just sit at your home and wonder why you don't have friends." - #LaGringa

Day 231: Today's Date: ___/___/____

I am _____

I am _____

I am _____

I am _____

I am _____

I am _____

I am _____

I am _____

I am _____

I am _____

I am _____

I am _____

I am _____

I am _____

I am _____

I _____

I _____

I _____

I _____

I _____

"Get attention by being attentive." - #LaGringa

Day 232: Today's Date: ___/___/____

I am _____

I am _____

I am _____

I am _____

I am _____

I am _____

I am _____

I am _____

I am _____

I am _____

I am _____

I am _____

I am _____

I am _____

I am _____

I _____

I _____

I _____

I _____

I _____

"TELL people who you are." - #LaGringa

Day 233: Today's Date: ___/___/____

I am _____

I am _____

I am _____

I am _____

I am _____

I am _____

I am _____

I am _____

I am _____

I am _____

I am _____

I am _____

I am _____

I am _____

I am _____

I _____

I _____

I _____

I _____

I _____

"People don't know who you are yet because you're not shouting loud enough. SCREAM IT LOUD IN THEIR FACE!" - #LaGringa

Day 234: Today's Date: ___/___/____

I am _____

I am _____

I am _____

I am _____

I am _____

I am _____

I am _____

I am _____

I am _____

I am _____

I am _____

I am _____

I am _____

I am _____

I am _____

I _____

I _____

I _____

I _____

I _____

"Be omnipresent where you want to be noticed." - #LaGringa

Day 235: Today's Date: ___/___/____

I am _____

I am _____

I am _____

I am _____

I am _____

I am _____

I am _____

I am _____

I am _____

I am _____

I am _____

I am _____

I am _____

I am _____

I am _____

I _____

I _____

I _____

I _____

I _____

"You have to be the one to start it. What is <u>it</u>?"- #LaGringa

Day 236: Today's Date: ___/___/____

I am _____

I am _____

I am _____

I am _____

I am _____

I am _____

I am _____

I am _____

I am _____

I am _____

I am _____

I am _____

I am _____

I am _____

I am _____

I _____

I _____

I _____

I _____

I _____

"Don't let anyone put a limit on your success, find a way above the ceiling."
- #LaGringa

Day 237: Today's Date: ___/___/____

I am _____

I am _____

I am _____

I am _____

I am _____

I am _____

I am _____

I am _____

I am _____

I am _____

I am _____

I am _____

I am _____

I am _____

I am _____

I _____

I _____

I _____

I _____

I _____

"Love is….. _____." - #LaGringa

Day 238: Today's Date: ___/___/____

I am _____

I am _____

I am _____

I am _____

I am _____

I am _____

I am _____

I am _____

I am _____

I am _____

I am _____

I am _____

I am _____

I am _____

I am _____

I _____

I _____

I _____

I _____

I _____

"Be yourself. Build a brand." - #LaGringa

Day 239: Today's Date: ___/___/____

I am _____

I am _____

I am _____

I am _____

I am _____

I am _____

I am _____

I am _____

I am _____

I am _____

I am _____

I am _____

I am _____

I am _____

I am _____

I _____

I _____

I _____

I _____

I _____

"I do my best thinking in the shower." - #LaGringa

Day 240: Today's Date: ___/___/____

I am _____

I am _____

I am _____

I am _____

I am _____

I am _____

I am _____

I am _____

I am _____

I am _____

I am _____

I am _____

I am _____

I am _____

I am _____

I _____

I _____

I _____

I _____

I _____

CONGRATULATIONS!!!

HOW DO YOU FEEL? BECAUSE YOU LOOK AWESOME!!!!!

You've completed 8 straight times of 30 day runs of committing to I am statements every morning. Look at that! You can do MORE than you think you can. Every day one step in the right direction. You are CHANGING YOUR LIFE! Take some time to reflect. Recognizing your growth and being intentional in your plans will help you to get the most out of this practice!

On Days 210 – 240 …

Did you WRITE every day? _____

Did you RECITE every day? _____

Did you LIGHT the World on fire every day? _____

Which of these three steps could you improve most in? How will you implement that moving forward?

What has changed for you over the past 30 days? What progress have you made? (Tip: Compare your day 210/211/212 journal entries to you most recent)

What would you like to get out of the NEXT 30 days?

BOOM. 2/3 of the day through your THIRD 90 DAY RUN – That's strong!

"Take time to notice the people around you." - #LaGringa

Day 241: Today's Date: ___/___/___

I am _____

I am _____

I am _____

I am _____

I am _____

I am _____

I am _____

I am _____

I am _____

I am _____

I am _____

I am _____

I am _____

I am _____

I am _____

I _____

I _____

I _____

I _____

I _____

"INTEND to grow today." - #LaGringa

Day 242: Today's Date: ___/___/____

I am _____

I am _____

I am _____

I am _____

I am _____

I am _____

I am _____

I am _____

I am _____

I am _____

I am _____

I am _____

I am _____

I am _____

I am _____

I _____

I _____

I _____

I _____

I _____

"Live like a ROCK STAR because you ARE one." - #LaGringa

Day 243: Today's Date: ___/___/___

I am _____

I am _____

I am _____

I am _____

I am _____

I am _____

I am _____

I am _____

I am _____

I am _____

I am _____

I am _____

I am _____

I am _____

I am _____

I _____

I _____

I _____

I _____

I _____

"Creo que tienes algo asombroso." - #LaGringa

Day 244: Today's Date: ___/___/___

I am _____

I am _____

I am _____

I am _____

I am _____

I am _____

I am _____

I am _____

I am _____

I am _____

I am _____

I am _____

I am _____

I am _____

I am _____

I _____

I _____

I _____

I _____

I _____

"If you were unstoppable what would you be doing differently?" - #LaGringa

Day 245: Today's Date: ___/___/___

I am _____

I am _____

I am _____

I am _____

I am _____

I am _____

I am _____

I am _____

I am _____

I am _____

I am _____

I am _____

I am _____

I am _____

I am _____

I _____

I _____

I _____

I _____

I _____

"Let your mind be a blank space for 10 minutes a day." - #LaGringa

Day 246: Today's Date: ___/___/____

I am _____

I am _____

I am _____

I am _____

I am _____

I am _____

I am _____

I am _____

I am _____

I am _____

I am _____

I am _____

I am _____

I am _____

I am _____

I _____

I _____

I _____

I _____

I _____

"Si crees que puedes entonces tienes razón." - #LaGringa

Day 247: Today's Date: ___/___/____

I am _____

I am _____

I am _____

I am _____

I am _____

I am _____

I am _____

I am _____

I am _____

I am _____

I am _____

I am _____

I am _____

I am _____

I am _____

I _____

I _____

I _____

I _____

I _____

"Let yourself be out of control today." - #LaGringa

Day 248: Today's Date: ___/___/____

I am _____

I am _____

I am _____

I am _____

I am _____

I am _____

I am _____

I am _____

I am _____

I am _____

I am _____

I am _____

I am _____

I am _____

I am _____

I _____

I _____

I _____

I _____

I _____

"There is no ceiling, no maximum, no limit." - #LaGringa

Day 249: Today's Date: ___/___/____

I am _____

I am _____

I am _____

I am _____

I am _____

I am _____

I am _____

I am _____

I am _____

I am _____

I am _____

I am _____

I am _____

I am _____

I am _____

I _____

I _____

I _____

I _____

I _____

"What if you just DID whatever you think you can't do?" - #LaGringa

Day 250: Today's Date: ___/___/____

I am _____

I am _____

I am _____

I am _____

I am _____

I am _____

I am _____

I am _____

I am _____

I am _____

I am _____

I am _____

I am _____

I am _____

I am _____

I am _____

I _____

I _____

I _____

I _____

I _____

"Me gustas." - #LaGringa

Day 251: Today's Date: ___/___/___

I am _____

I am _____

I am _____

I am _____

I am _____

I am _____

I am _____

I am _____

I am _____

I am _____

I am _____

I am _____

I am _____

I am _____

I am _____

I _____

I _____

I _____

I _____

I _____

"Might as well just do it. Might as well keep going." - #LaGringa

Day 252: Today's Date: ___/___/____

I am _____

I am _____

I am _____

I am _____

I am _____

I am _____

I am _____

I am _____

I am _____

I am _____

I am _____

I am _____

I am _____

I am _____

I am _____

I _____

I _____

I _____

I _____

I _____

"Everyone has the same fears you do." - #LaGringa

Day 253: Today's Date: ___/___/____

I am _____

I am _____

I am _____

I am _____

I am _____

I am _____

I am _____

I am _____

I am _____

I am _____

I am _____

I am _____

I am _____

I am _____

I am _____

I _____

I _____

I _____

I _____

I _____

"Assume the positive." - #LaGringa

Day 254: Today's Date: ___/___/____

I am _____

I am _____

I am _____

I am _____

I am _____

I am _____

I am _____

I am _____

I am _____

I am _____

I am _____

I am _____

I am _____

I am _____

I am _____

I _____

I _____

I _____

I _____

I _____

"Be the starter. No room for second string in your life." - #LaGringa

Day 255: Today's Date: ___/___/____

I am _____

I am _____

I am _____

I am _____

I am _____

I am _____

I am _____

I am _____

I am _____

I am _____

I am _____

I am _____

I am _____

I am _____

I am _____

I _____

I _____

I _____

I _____

I _____

"256 is my lucky number. What is yours?" - #LaGringa

Day 256: Today's Date: ___/___/____

I am _____

I am _____

I am _____

I am _____

I am _____

I am _____

I am _____

I am _____

I am _____

I am _____

I am _____

I am _____

I am _____

I am _____

I am _____

I _____

I _____

I _____

I _____

I _____

"Recognizing your negative patterns is how you start to break them." - #LaGringa

Day 257: Today's Date: ___/___/____

I am _____

I am _____

I am _____

I am _____

I am _____

I am _____

I am _____

I am _____

I am _____

I am _____

I am _____

I am _____

I am _____

I am _____

I am _____

I _____

I _____

I _____

I _____

I _____

"Embrace being sucky at something. That means you're growing!" - #LaGringa

Day 258: Today's Date: ___/___/____

I am _____

I am _____

I am _____

I am _____

I am _____

I am _____

I am _____

I am _____

I am _____

I am _____

I am _____

I am _____

I am _____

I am _____

I am _____

I _____

I _____

I _____

I _____

I _____

"No one expects you to be perfect, in fact they think that's weird." - #LaGringa

Day 259: Today's Date: ___/___/____

I am _____

I am _____

I am _____

I am _____

I am _____

I am _____

I am _____

I am _____

I am _____

I am _____

I am _____

I am _____

I am _____

I am _____

I am _____

I _____

I _____

I _____

I _____

I _____

"Be part of the revolution." - #LaGringa

Day 260: Today's Date: ___/___/____

I am _____

I am _____

I am _____

I am _____

I am _____

I am _____

I am _____

I am _____

I am _____

I am _____

I am _____

I am _____

I am _____

I am _____

I am _____

I _____

I _____

I _____

I _____

I _____

"Find the future. Be the future." - #LaGringa

Day 261: Today's Date: ___/___/____

I am _____

I am _____

I am _____

I am _____

I am _____

I am _____

I am _____

I am _____

I am _____

I am _____

I am _____

I am _____

I am _____

I am _____

I am _____

I _____

I _____

I _____

I _____

I _____

"Anything is the right thing to do if it's the thing you are doing." - #LaGringa

Day 262: Today's Date: ___/___/____

I am _____

I am _____

I am _____

I am _____

I am _____

I am _____

I am _____

I am _____

I am _____

I am _____

I am _____

I am _____

I am _____

I am _____

I am _____

I _____

I _____

I _____

I _____

I _____

"You gotta grind." - #LaGringa

Day 263: Today's Date: ___/___/____

I am _____

I am _____

I am _____

I am _____

I am _____

I am _____

I am _____

I am _____

I am _____

I am _____

I am _____

I am _____

I am _____

I am _____

I am _____

I _____

I _____

I _____

I _____

I _____

"Do you know where you're going? Because if not, you're already there."
- #LaGringa

Day 264: Today's Date: ___/___/____

I am _____

I am _____

I am _____

I am _____

I am _____

I am _____

I am _____

I am _____

I am _____

I am _____

I am _____

I am _____

I am _____

I am _____

I am _____

I _____

I _____

I _____

I _____

I _____

"What is holding your back? Break through it." - #LaGringa

Day 265: Today's Date: ___/___/____

I am _____

I am _____

I am _____

I am _____

I am _____

I am _____

I am _____

I am _____

I am _____

I am _____

I am _____

I am _____

I am _____

I am _____

I am _____

I _____

I _____

I _____

I _____

I _____

"Everyone sounds stupid, so don't be afraid to. Speak your mind." - #LaGringa

Day 266: Today's Date: ___/___/____

I am _____

I am _____

I am _____

I am _____

I am _____

I am _____

I am _____

I am _____

I am _____

I am _____

I am _____

I am _____

I am _____

I am _____

I am _____

I _____

I _____

I _____

I _____

I _____

"It's OK to think you're IMPORTANT, because YOU ARE." - #LaGringa

Day 267: Today's Date: ___/___/____

I am _____

I am _____

I am _____

I am _____

I am _____

I am _____

I am _____

I am _____

I am _____

I am _____

I am _____

I am _____

I am _____

I am _____

I am _____

I _____

I _____

I _____

I _____

I _____

"Look in the mirror and say you have all the reasons to be full of yourself!!!! "
- #LaGringa

Day 268: Today's Date: ___/___/____

I am _____

I am _____

I am _____

I am _____

I am _____

I am _____

I am _____

I am _____

I am _____

I am _____

I am _____

I am _____

I am _____

I am _____

I am _____

I _____

I _____

I _____

I _____

I _____

"Be with someone that says we." - #LaGringa

Day 269: Today's Date: ___/___/____

I am _____

I am _____

I am _____

I am _____

I am _____

I am _____

I am _____

I am _____

I am _____

I am _____

I am _____

I am _____

I am _____

I am _____

I am _____

I _____

I _____

I _____

I _____

I _____

"Where is your happiest place on earth?." - #LaGringa

Day 270: Today's Date: ___/___/____

I am _____

I am _____

I am _____

I am _____

I am _____

I am _____

I am _____

I am _____

I am _____

I am _____

I am _____

I am _____

I am _____

I am _____

I am _____

I _____

I _____

I _____

I _____

I _____

CONGRATULATIONS!!!

I'M FALLING IN LOVE WITH YOU!

You've completed 9 straight times of 30 day runs of committing to I am statements every morning. HOLY WOW!!!! That is THREE 90 day RUNS!!!!! You are UNSTOPPABLE. Every day one step in the right direction. You are CHANGING YOUR LIFE! Take some time to reflect. Recognizing your growth and being intentional in your plans will help you to get the most out of this practice!

On Days 240 - 270 …

Did you WRITE every day? _____

Did you RECITE every day? _____

Did you LIGHT the World on fire every day? _____

Which of these three steps could you improve most in? How will you implement that moving forward?

Let's look back at your last 90 day Run - What has changed for you over the past 90 days? What progress have you made? (Tip: Compare your day 90/91/92 journal entries to you most recent)

What would you like to get out of the <u>NEXT</u> 30 days?

HERE WE GOOOOOOOOOOOOOOOOO!!!!!!!!!!

STOP and fill out this page BEFORE moving forward.

Has this practice been impactful for you in the last 90 days?

(circle one)

YES   No   YES   Maybe   YES

If you circled YES... LOOK AT YOU ROCKIN IT!!!! Now it is time to pay it forward. What if you could change 5 people's lives EVERY 90 days? You can. And you have been!!!! You have impacted 10 people so far by sharing this book – WOW YOU ROCK!!!!! Whether you see it right now or not I am confident you had a MAJOR impact in their life. Now YOU have the power to change MORE people's lives simply by sharing this book with them!!!! It is time to impact the WORLD, again.

Who are 5 people in your life that you think could benefit from this practice?

1. _____
2. _____
3. _____
4. _____
5. _____

What can you do to make sure that they get a new copy of this journal in the next 10 days?

Meet up for coffee and explain to them how much this has impacted you

Send them a link to purchase the book on Amazon

Post it on Social media and tag them

Send them a text message about how impactful it has been for you

Hand write a letter to them about the impact and send it in the mail

Purchase them a copy as a gift

If you circled Maybe...

Have you honestly committed EVERY morning for the last 30 days straight?

What is causing you to waiver in your feelings towards this daily practice?

What could YOU do to turn your answer into a YES?

If you circled No...

Have you honestly committed EVERY morning for the last 30 days straight?

What about the exercise is making you feel uncomfortable?

How could you turn it around and make it impact the NEXT 30 days of your life?

"Connect with humanity." - #LaGringa

Day 271: Today's Date: ___/___/___

I am _____

I am _____

I am _____

I am _____

I am _____

I am _____

I am _____

I am _____

I am _____

I am _____

I am _____

I am _____

I am _____

I am _____

I am _____

I _____

I _____

I _____

I _____

I _____

"This IS the real World." - #LaGringa

Day 272: Today's Date: ___/___/____

I am _____

I am _____

I am _____

I am _____

I am _____

I am _____

I am _____

I am _____

I am _____

I am _____

I am _____

I am _____

I am _____

I am _____

I am _____

I _____

I _____

I _____

I _____

I _____

"You can't be who you are without other people." - #LaGringa

Day 273: Today's Date: ___/___/____

I am _____

I am _____

I am _____

I am _____

I am _____

I am _____

I am _____

I am _____

I am _____

I am _____

I am _____

I am _____

I am _____

I am _____

I am _____

I am _____

I _____

I _____

I _____

I _____

I _____

"The answer to your problem might be in the mind of the person right next to you." - #LaGringa

Day 274: Today's Date: ___/___/____

I am _____

I am _____

I am _____

I am _____

I am _____

I am _____

I am _____

I am _____

I am _____

I am _____

I am _____

I am _____

I am _____

I am _____

I am _____

I _____

I _____

I _____

I _____

I _____

"Maybe the world needs you to suck so they can have the confident to have courage to do it too." - #LaGringa

Day 275: Today's Date: ___/___/____

I am _____

I am _____

I am _____

I am _____

I am _____

I am _____

I am _____

I am _____

I am _____

I am _____

I am _____

I am _____

I am _____

I am _____

I am _____

I _____

I _____

I _____

I _____

I _____

"Show people what you are doing." - #LaGringa

Day 276: Today's Date: ___/___/____

I am _____

I am _____

I am _____

I am _____

I am _____

I am _____

I am _____

I am _____

I am _____

I am _____

I am _____

I am _____

I am _____

I am _____

I am _____

I _____

I _____

I _____

I _____

I _____

"You DO have something good to say." - #LaGringa

Day 277: Today's Date: ___/___/____

I am _____

I am _____

I am _____

I am _____

I am _____

I am _____

I am _____

I am _____

I am _____

I am _____

I am _____

I am _____

I am _____

I am _____

I am _____

I _____

I _____

I _____

I _____

I _____

"I do this for YOU. Myself." - #LaGringa

Day 278: Today's Date: ___/___/____

I am _____

I am _____

I am _____

I am _____

I am _____

I am _____

I am _____

I am _____

I am _____

I am _____

I am _____

I am _____

I am _____

I am _____

I am _____

I _____

I _____

I _____

I _____

I _____

"You don't need to be revolutionary to be impactful." - #LaGringa

Day 279: Today's Date: ___/___/____

I am _____

I am _____

I am _____

I am _____

I am _____

I am _____

I am _____

I am _____

I am _____

I am _____

I am _____

I am _____

I am _____

I am _____

I am _____

I _____

I _____

I _____

I _____

I _____

"You're beautiful and amazing and I love you." - #LaGringa

Day 280: Today's Date: ___/___/____

I am _____

I am _____

I am _____

I am _____

I am _____

I am _____

I am _____

I am _____

I am _____

I am _____

I am _____

I am _____

I am _____

I am _____

I am _____

I _____

I _____

I _____

I _____

I _____

"Courage is courageous." - #LaGringa

Day 281: Today's Date: ___/___/____

I am _____

I am _____

I am _____

I am _____

I am _____

I am _____

I am _____

I am _____

I am _____

I am _____

I am _____

I am _____

I am _____

I am _____

I am _____

I _____

I _____

I _____

I _____

I _____

"OMG!!!... You're right." - #LaGringa

Day 282: Today's Date: ___/___/____

I am _____

I am _____

I am _____

I am _____

I am _____

I am _____

I am _____

I am _____

I am _____

I am _____

I am _____

I am _____

I am _____

I am _____

I am _____

I _____

I _____

I _____

I _____

I _____

"Talk positively to your future self." - #LaGringa

Day 283: Today's Date: ___/___/____

I am _____

I am _____

I am _____

I am _____

I am _____

I am _____

I am _____

I am _____

I am _____

I am _____

I am _____

I am _____

I am _____

I am _____

I am _____

I _____

I _____

I _____

I _____

I _____

"All really massively successful people are crazy. So stay crazy. Keep it NUTS."
- #LaGringa

Day 284: Today's Date: ___/___/____

I am _____

I am _____

I am _____

I am _____

I am _____

I am _____

I am _____

I am _____

I am _____

I am _____

I am _____

I am _____

I am _____

I am _____

I am _____

I _____

I _____

I _____

I _____

I _____

"If you ask someone do to something enough times eventually they will."
- #LaGringa

Day 285: Today's Date: ___/___/____

I am _____

I am _____

I am _____

I am _____

I am _____

I am _____

I am _____

I am _____

I am _____

I am _____

I am _____

I am _____

I am _____

I am _____

I am _____

I _____

I _____

I _____

I _____

I _____

"Surround yourself with people who support you." - #LaGringa

Day 286: Today's Date: ___/___/____

I am _____

I am _____

I am _____

I am _____

I am _____

I am _____

I am _____

I am _____

I am _____

I am _____

I am _____

I am _____

I am _____

I am _____

I am _____

I _____

I _____

I _____

I _____

I _____

"Don't be afraid just because you think you're supposed to be afriad." - #LaGringa

Day 287: Today's Date: ___/___/____

I am _____

I am _____

I am _____

I am _____

I am _____

I am _____

I am _____

I am _____

I am _____

I am _____

I am _____

I am _____

I am _____

I am _____

I am _____

I am _____

I _____

I _____

I _____

I _____

I _____

"GROW through sharing." - #LaGringa

Day 288: Today's Date: ___/___/____

I am _____

I am _____

I am _____

I am _____

I am _____

I am _____

I am _____

I am _____

I am _____

I am _____

I am _____

I am _____

I am _____

I am _____

I am _____

I _____

I _____

I _____

I _____

I _____

"Don't put anger to sleep in your heart." - #LaGringa

Day 289: Today's Date: ___/___/____

I am _____

I am _____

I am _____

I am _____

I am _____

I am _____

I am _____

I am _____

I am _____

I am _____

I am _____

I am _____

I am _____

I am _____

I am _____

I _____

I _____

I _____

I _____

I _____

"Sleep sweet." - #LaGringa

Day 290: Today's Date: ___/___/____

I am _____

I am _____

I am _____

I am _____

I am _____

I am _____

I am _____

I am _____

I am _____

I am _____

I am _____

I am _____

I am _____

I am _____

I am _____

I _____

I _____

I _____

I _____

I _____

"Treat yourself to something naughty." - #LaGringa

Day 291: Today's Date: ___/___/____

I am _____

I am _____

I am _____

I am _____

I am _____

I am _____

I am _____

I am _____

I am _____

I am _____

I am _____

I am _____

I am _____

I am _____

I am _____

I _____

I _____

I _____

I _____

I _____

"You can't make today go away, so go IN." - #LaGringa

Day 292: Today's Date: ___/___/____

I am _____

I am _____

I am _____

I am _____

I am _____

I am _____

I am _____

I am _____

I am _____

I am _____

I am _____

I am _____

I am _____

I am _____

I am _____

I _____

I _____

I _____

I _____

I _____

"You are not a child anymore. Deal with it." - #LaGringa

Day 293: Today's Date: ___/___/____

I am _____

I am _____

I am _____

I am _____

I am _____

I am _____

I am _____

I am _____

I am _____

I am _____

I am _____

I am _____

I am _____

I am _____

I am _____

I am _____

I _____

I _____

I _____

I _____

I _____

"Break that shhhh….." - #LaGringa

Day 294: Today's Date: ___/___/____

I am _____

I am _____

I am _____

I am _____

I am _____

I am _____

I am _____

I am _____

I am _____

I am _____

I am _____

I am _____

I am _____

I am _____

I am _____

I _____

I _____

I _____

I _____

I _____

"Put good thoughts in your head." - #LaGringa

Day 295: Today's Date: ___/___/____

I am _____

I am _____

I am _____

I am _____

I am _____

I am _____

I am _____

I am _____

I am _____

I am _____

I am _____

I am _____

I am _____

I am _____

I am _____

I _____

I _____

I _____

I _____

I _____

"Don't focus on what got you here. Focus on what will get you there." - #LaGringa

Day 296: Today's Date: ___/___/____

I am _____

I am _____

I am _____

I am _____

I am _____

I am _____

I am _____

I am _____

I am _____

I am _____

I am _____

I am _____

I am _____

I am _____

I am _____

I _____

I _____

I _____

I _____

I _____

"Make an inner discovery." - #LaGringa

Day 297: Today's Date: ___/___/____

I am _____

I am _____

I am _____

I am _____

I am _____

I am _____

I am _____

I am _____

I am _____

I am _____

I am _____

I am _____

I am _____

I am _____

I am _____

I _____

I _____

I _____

I _____

I _____

"ONLY play music that inspires your mind." - #LaGringa

Day 298: Today's Date: ___/___/___

I am _____

I am _____

I am _____

I am _____

I am _____

I am _____

I am _____

I am _____

I am _____

I am _____

I am _____

I am _____

I am _____

I am _____

I am _____

I _____

I _____

I _____

I _____

I _____

"Live in line with your intentions." - #LaGringa

Day 299: Today's Date: ___/___/___

I am _____

I am _____

I am _____

I am _____

I am _____

I am _____

I am _____

I am _____

I am _____

I am _____

I am _____

I am _____

I am _____

I am _____

I _____

I _____

I _____

I _____

I _____

"Tomorrow never comes." - #LaGringa

Day 300: Today's Date: ___/___/____

I am _____

I am _____

I am _____

I am _____

I am _____

I am _____

I am _____

I am _____

I am _____

I am _____

I am _____

I am _____

I am _____

I am _____

I am _____

I _____

I _____

I _____

I _____

I _____

CONGRATULATIONS!!!

HOLY MOLY!!!! YOU ARE THE BEES KNEES!!!

You've completed 10 straight times of 30 day runs of committing to I am statements every morning. 300 is a quite a number my friend! You are shining from head to toe! Every day one step in the right direction. You are CHANGING YOUR LIFE! Take some time to reflect. Recognizing your growth and being intentional in your plans will help you to get the most out of this practice!

On Days 270 - 300 …

Did you WRITE every day? _____

Did you RECITE every day? _____

Did you LIGHT the World on fire every day? _____

Which of these three steps could you improve most in? How will you implement that moving forward?

What has changed for you over the past 30 days? What progress have you made? (Tip: Compare your day 270/271/272 journal entries to you most recent)

What would you like to get out of the <u>NEXT</u> 30 days?

YOU… YOU ARE IMPRESSIVE MY FRIEND!!!

"Copy and paste." - #LaGringa

Day 301: Today's Date: ___/___/____

I am _____

I am _____

I am _____

I am _____

I am _____

I am _____

I am _____

I am _____

I am _____

I am _____

I am _____

I am _____

I am _____

I am _____

I am _____

I _____

I _____

I _____

I _____

I _____

"Create a solution and write it down." - #LaGringa

Day 302: Today's Date: ___/___/____

I am _____

I am _____

I am _____

I am _____

I am _____

I am _____

I am _____

I am _____

I am _____

I am _____

I am _____

I am _____

I am _____

I am _____

I am _____

I _____

I _____

I _____

I _____

I _____

**"When you bury something inside of your heart it starts to decay and rot."
- #LaGringa**

Day 303: Today's Date: ___/___/____

I am _____

I am _____

I am _____

I am _____

I am _____

I am _____

I am _____

I am _____

I am _____

I am _____

I am _____

I am _____

I am _____

I am _____

I am _____

I _____

I _____

I _____

I _____

I _____

"Don't ever go to bed upset, angry or in turmoil. Going to sleep does not fix your problem it only engrains it in your subconscious." - #LaGringa

Day 304: Today's Date: ___/___/___

I am _____

I am _____

I am _____

I am _____

I am _____

I am _____

I am _____

I am _____

I am _____

I am _____

I am _____

I am _____

I am _____

I am _____

I am _____

I _____

I _____

I _____

I _____

I _____

"Challenge the truth of your DEFINITE truths and thoughts." - #LaGringa

Day 305: Today's Date: ___/___/____

I am _____

I am _____

I am _____

I am _____

I am _____

I am _____

I am _____

I am _____

I am _____

I am _____

I am _____

I am _____

I am _____

I am _____

I am _____

I _____

I _____

I _____

I _____

I _____

"Deal with your problems when are you conscious." - #LaGringa

Day 306: Today's Date: ___/___/____

I am _____

I am _____

I am _____

I am _____

I am _____

I am _____

I am _____

I am _____

I am _____

I am _____

I am _____

I am _____

I am _____

I am _____

I am _____

I _____

I _____

I _____

I _____

I _____

"When you go to sleep with hurt it just stays there. Stay awake and work it out."
- #LaGringa

Day 307: Today's Date: ___/___/____

I am _____

I am _____

I am _____

I am _____

I am _____

I am _____

I am _____

I am _____

I am _____

I am _____

I am _____

I am _____

I am _____

I am _____

I am _____

I _____

I _____

I _____

I _____

I _____

"No puedes retener el tiempo solo puedes usarlo." - #LaGringa

Day 308: Today's Date: ___/___/____

I am _____

I am _____

I am _____

I am _____

I am _____

I am _____

I am _____

I am _____

I am _____

I am _____

I am _____

I am _____

I am _____

I am _____

I am _____

I _____

I _____

I _____

I _____

I _____

"Get up on their shit." - #LaGringa

Day 309: Today's Date: ___/___/____

I am _____

I am _____

I am _____

I am _____

I am _____

I am _____

I am _____

I am _____

I am _____

I am _____

I am _____

I am _____

I am _____

I am _____

I am _____

I _____

I _____

I _____

I _____

I _____

"Quiero ser tu amigo." - #LaGringa

Day 310: Today's Date: ___/___/____

I am _____

I am _____

I am _____

I am _____

I am _____

I am _____

I am _____

I am _____

I am _____

I am _____

I am _____

I am _____

I am _____

I am _____

I am _____

I _____

I _____

I _____

I _____

I _____

"Live life by design." - #LaGringa

Day 311: Today's Date: ___/___/___

I am _____

I am _____

I am _____

I am _____

I am _____

I am _____

I am _____

I am _____

I am _____

I am _____

I am _____

I am _____

I am _____

I am _____

I am _____

I _____

I _____

I _____

I _____

I _____

"Overtake time." - #LaGringa

Day 312: Today's Date: ___/___/____

I am _____

I am _____

I am _____

I am _____

I am _____

I am _____

I am _____

I am _____

I am _____

I am _____

I am _____

I am _____

I am _____

I am _____

I am _____

I _____

I _____

I _____

I _____

I _____

"Listen to how you speak about time." - #LaGringa

Day 313: Today's Date: ___/___/____

I am _____

I am _____

I am _____

I am _____

I am _____

I am _____

I am _____

I am _____

I am _____

I am _____

I am _____

I am _____

I am _____

I am _____

I am _____

I _____

I _____

I _____

I _____

I _____

"Choose your language carefully." - #LaGringa

Day 314: Today's Date: ___/___/____

I am _____

I am _____

I am _____

I am _____

I am _____

I am _____

I am _____

I am _____

I am _____

I am _____

I am _____

I am _____

I am _____

I am _____

I am _____

I _____

I _____

I _____

I _____

I _____

"Your language dictates your experience." - #LaGringa

Day 315: Today's Date: ___/___/____

I am _____

I am _____

I am _____

I am _____

I am _____

I am _____

I am _____

I am _____

I am _____

I am _____

I am _____

I am _____

I am _____

I am _____

I am _____

I _____

I _____

I _____

I _____

I _____

"Give yourself ownership." - #LaGringa

Day 316: Today's Date: ___/___/____

I am _____

I am _____

I am _____

I am _____

I am _____

I am _____

I am _____

I am _____

I am _____

I am _____

I am _____

I am _____

I am _____

I am _____

I am _____

I _____

I _____

I _____

I _____

I _____

"_____ and chill. How you fill the blank will determine your life."
- #LaGringa

Day 317: Today's Date: ___/___/____

I am _____

I am _____

I am _____

I am _____

I am _____

I am _____

I am _____

I am _____

I am _____

I am _____

I am _____

I am _____

I am _____

I am _____

I am _____

I _____

I _____

I _____

I _____

I _____

"Limpia tu vida ." - #LaGringa

Day 318: Today's Date: ___/___/____

I am _____

I am _____

I am _____

I am _____

I am _____

I am _____

I am _____

I am _____

I am _____

I am _____

I am _____

I am _____

I am _____

I am _____

I am _____

I _____

I _____

I _____

I _____

I _____

"If you don't love it, throw it out." - #LaGringa

Day 319: Today's Date: ___/___/____

I am _____

I am _____

I am _____

I am _____

I am _____

I am _____

I am _____

I am _____

I am _____

I am _____

I am _____

I am _____

I am _____

I am _____

I am _____

I _____

I _____

I _____

I _____

I _____

"How often do you review your notes?" - #LaGringa

Day 320: Today's Date: ___/___/____

I am _____

I am _____

I am _____

I am _____

I am _____

I am _____

I am _____

I am _____

I am _____

I am _____

I am _____

I am _____

I am _____

I am _____

I am _____

I _____

I _____

I _____

I _____

I _____

"Take notes like a mad person." - #LaGringa

Day 321: Today's Date: ___/___/____

I am _____

I am _____

I am _____

I am _____

I am _____

I am _____

I am _____

I am _____

I am _____

I am _____

I am _____

I am _____

I am _____

I am _____

I am _____

I _____

I _____

I _____

I _____

I _____

"Need more than other people." - #LaGringa

Day 322: Today's Date: ___/___/____

I am _____

I am _____

I am _____

I am _____

I am _____

I am _____

I am _____

I am _____

I am _____

I am _____

I am _____

I am _____

I am _____

I am _____

I am _____

I _____

I _____

I _____

I _____

I _____

"If a customer is flirting with your product, you can close the deal." - #LaGringa

Day 323: Today's Date: ___/___/____

I am _____

I am _____

I am _____

I am _____

I am _____

I am _____

I am _____

I am _____

I am _____

I am _____

I am _____

I am _____

I am _____

I am _____

I am _____

I _____

I _____

I _____

I _____

I _____

"Your life is more important than you are making it." - #LaGringa

Day 324: Today's Date: ___/___/____

I am _____

I am _____

I am _____

I am _____

I am _____

I am _____

I am _____

I am _____

I am _____

I am _____

I am _____

I am _____

I am _____

I am _____

I am _____

I _____

I _____

I _____

I _____

I _____

"Watch good stuff on replay. Watch good stuff on replay." - #LaGringa

Day 325: Today's Date: ___/___/____

I am _____

I am _____

I am _____

I am _____

I am _____

I am _____

I am _____

I am _____

I am _____

I am _____

I am _____

I am _____

I am _____

I am _____

I am _____

I _____

I _____

I _____

I _____

I _____

"Take care of your surroundings." - #LaGringa

Day 326: Today's Date: ___/___/____

I am _____

I am _____

I am _____

I am _____

I am _____

I am _____

I am _____

I am _____

I am _____

I am _____

I am _____

I am _____

I am _____

I am _____

I am _____

I _____

I _____

I _____

I _____

I _____

"It doesn't have to be this way." - #LaGringa

Day 327: Today's Date: ___/___/____

I am _____

I am _____

I am _____

I am _____

I am _____

I am _____

I am _____

I am _____

I am _____

I am _____

I am _____

I am _____

I am _____

I am _____

I am _____

I am _____

I _____

I _____

I _____

I _____

I _____

"Have a revelation today." - #LaGringa

Day 328: Today's Date: ___/___/____

I am _____

I am _____

I am _____

I am _____

I am _____

I am _____

I am _____

I am _____

I am _____

I am _____

I am _____

I am _____

I am _____

I am _____

I am _____

I _____

I _____

I _____

I _____

I _____

"If you get momentum going, don't break it. Ride the wave." - #LaGringa

Day 329: Today's Date: ___/___/____

I am _____

I am _____

I am _____

I am _____

I am _____

I am _____

I am _____

I am _____

I am _____

I am _____

I am _____

I am _____

I am _____

I am _____

I am _____

I _____

I _____

I _____

I _____

I _____

"Make someone your MVP and tell the World." - #LaGringa

Day 330: Today's Date: ___/___/____

I am _____

I am _____

I am _____

I am _____

I am _____

I am _____

I am _____

I am _____

I am _____

I am _____

I am _____

I am _____

I am _____

I am _____

I am _____

I _____

I _____

I _____

I _____

I _____

CONGRATULATIONS!!!

I OFFICIALLY LOVE YOU!!!

You've completed 30 day runs of committing to I am statements every morning 11 times in a row. You should be SOOOO incredibly proud of yourself. You're life is RAPIDLY CHANGING!!! Take some time to reflect. Recognizing your growth and being intentional in your plans will help you to get the most out of this practice!

On Days 300 – 330 …

Did you WRITE every day? _____

Did you RECITE every day? _____

Did you LIGHT the World on fire every day? _____

Which of these three steps could you improve most in? How will you implement that moving forward?

Let's look back at your last 90 day Run - What has changed for you over the past 90 days? What progress have you made? (Tip: Compare your day 90/91/92 journal entries to you most recent)

What would you like to get out of the <u>NEXT</u> 30 days?

HERE WE GOOOOOOOOOOOOOOOOO!!!!!!!!!!

"Never stop doing the things that make your eyes sparkle with joy"
-#LaGringa

Good news: You have completed almost an entire year of this amazing daily practice!!!

Great news: You don't have to stop at the end of the one year mark!

INCREDIBLE news: You can go online and purchase your next copy TODAY so that you don't have to even skip one day. Get the new copy in before you finish with this one!

Pick up your phone right now and go on Amazon! Just search "Janine Grant" and get your next copy in the mail to you today!!! ☺

"Be a person of your word. Especially the words you write below."
- #LaGringa

Day 331: Today's Date: ___/___/____

I am _____

I am _____

I am _____

I am _____

I am _____

I am _____

I am _____

I am _____

I am _____

I am _____

I am _____

I am _____

I am _____

I am _____

I am _____

I _____

I _____

I _____

I _____

I _____

"Put yourself in the environment to be successful. Even if you don't have the energy to take the actions, be in the space." - #LaGringa

Day 332: Today's Date: ___/___/____

I am _____

I am _____

I am _____

I am _____

I am _____

I am _____

I am _____

I am _____

I am _____

I am _____

I am _____

I am _____

I am _____

I am _____

I am _____

I am _____

I _____

I _____

I _____

I _____

I _____

"Put stuff in your way to make you feel great." - #LaGringa

Day 333: Today's Date: ___/___/____

I am _____

I am _____

I am _____

I am _____

I am _____

I am _____

I am _____

I am _____

I am _____

I am _____

I am _____

I am _____

I am _____

I am _____

I am _____

I _____

I _____

I _____

I _____

I _____

"Take a chance and do something different today." - #LaGringa

Day 334: Today's Date: ___/___/____

I am _____

I am _____

I am _____

I am _____

I am _____

I am _____

I am _____

I am _____

I am _____

I am _____

I am _____

I am _____

I am _____

I am _____

I am _____

I _____

I _____

I _____

I _____

I _____

"Everyone experiences self-doubt. You can feel it, and give yourself confidence anyway!" - #LaGringa

Day 335: Today's Date: ___/___/____

I am _____ _____

I am _____

I am _____

I am _____

I am _____

I am _____

I am _____

I am _____

I am _____

I am _____

I am _____

I am _____

I am _____

I am _____

I am _____

I _____

I _____

I _____

I _____

I _____

"Where were you one year ago today? Where will you be one year from today?"
- #LaGringa

Day 336: Today's Date: ___/___/____

I am _____

I am _____

I am _____

I am _____

I am _____

I am _____

I am _____

I am _____

I am _____

I am _____

I am _____

I am _____

I am _____

I am _____

I am _____

I _____

I _____

I _____

I _____

I _____

"There is EVEN MORE greatness inside of you that you haven't tapped into yet."
- #LaGringa

Day 337: Today's Date: ___/___/____

I am _____

I am _____

I am _____

I am _____

I am _____

I am _____

I am _____

I am _____

I am _____

I am _____

I am _____

I am _____

I am _____

I am _____

I am _____

I _____

I _____

I _____

I _____

I _____

"YES. What you are thinking IS the right decision. DO IT." - #LaGringa

Day 338: Today's Date: ___/___/____

I am _____

I am _____

I am _____

I am _____

I am _____

I am _____

I am _____

I am _____

I am _____

I am _____

I am _____

I am _____

I am _____

I am _____

I am _____

I _____

I _____

I _____

I _____

I _____

"Trust yourself." - #LaGringa

Day 339: Today's Date: ___/___/___

I am _____

I am _____

I am _____

I am _____

I am _____

I am _____

I am _____

I am _____

I am _____

I am _____

I am _____

I am _____

I am _____

I am _____

I am _____

I _____

I _____

I _____

I _____

I _____

"Trust is an investment. You will be paid back with interest." - #LaGringa

Day 340: Today's Date: ___/___/____

I am _____

I am _____

I am _____

I am _____

I am _____

I am _____

I am _____

I am _____

I am _____

I am _____

I am _____

I am _____

I am _____

I am _____

I am _____

I _____

I _____

I _____

I _____

I _____

"Tell yourself what you need to hear." - #LaGringa

Day 341: Today's Date: ___/___/___

I am _____

I am _____

I am _____

I am _____

I am _____

I am _____

I am _____

I am _____

I am _____

I am _____

I am _____

I am _____

I am _____

I am _____

I am _____

I _____

I _____

I _____

I _____

I _____

"Find your tribe." - #LaGringa

Day 342: Today's Date: ___/___/____

I am _____

I am _____

I am _____

I am _____

I am _____

I am _____

I am _____

I am _____

I am _____

I am _____

I am _____

I am _____

I am _____

I am _____

I am _____

I _____

I _____

I _____

I _____

I _____

"Puedes hacerlo." - #LaGringa

Day 343: Today's Date: ___/___/____

I am _____

I am _____

I am _____

I am _____

I am _____

I am _____

I am _____

I am _____

I am _____

I am _____

I am _____

I am _____

I am _____

I am _____

I am _____

I _____

I _____

I _____

I _____

I _____

"Be appreciative of every moment in your life." - #LaGringa

Day 344: Today's Date: ___/___/____

I am _____

I am _____

I am _____

I am _____

I am _____

I am _____

I am _____

I am _____

I am _____

I am _____

I am _____

I am _____

I am _____

I am _____

I am _____

I _____

I _____

I _____

I _____

I _____

"Talk about happiness." - #LaGringa

Day 345: Today's Date: ___/___/____

I am _____

I am _____

I am _____

I am _____

I am _____

I am _____

I am _____

I am _____

I am _____

I am _____

I am _____

I am _____

I am _____

I am _____

I am _____

I _____

I _____

I _____

I _____

I _____

"Become the thing that people talk about." - #LaGringa

Day 346: Today's Date: ___/___/____

I am _____

I am _____

I am _____

I am _____

I am _____

I am _____

I am _____

I am _____

I am _____

I am _____

I am _____

I am _____

I am _____

I am _____

I am _____

I _____

I _____

I _____

I _____

I _____

"Work through the hurt." - #LaGringa

Day 347: Today's Date: ___/___/____

I am _____

I am _____

I am _____

I am _____

I am _____

I am _____

I am _____

I am _____

I am _____

I am _____

I am _____

I am _____

I am _____

I am _____

I am _____

I _____

I _____

I _____

I _____

I _____

"Challenge yourself. Challenge other people. You come first." - #LaGringa

Day 348: Today's Date: ___/___/____

I am _____

I am _____

I am _____

I am _____

I am _____

I am _____

I am _____

I am _____

I am _____

I am _____

I am _____

I am _____

I am _____

I am _____

I am _____

I _____

I _____

I _____

I _____

I _____

"People will love you if you let them." - #LaGringa

Day 349: Today's Date: ___/___/____

I am _____

I am _____

I am _____

I am _____

I am _____

I am _____

I am _____

I am _____

I am _____

I am _____

I am _____

I am _____

I am _____

I am _____

I am _____

I _____

I _____

I _____

I _____

I _____

"Camina en la dirección de tus sueños." - #LaGringa

Day 350: Today's Date: ___/___/____

I am _____

I am _____

I am _____

I am _____

I am _____

I am _____

I am _____

I am _____

I am _____

I am _____

I am _____

I am _____

I am _____

I am _____

I am _____

I _____

I _____

I _____

I _____

I _____

"Put yourself out there, let people judge you, and don't give a shit." - #LaGringa

Day 351: Today's Date: ___/___/____

I am _____

I am _____

I am _____

I am _____

I am _____

I am _____

I am _____

I am _____

I am _____

I am _____

I am _____

I am _____

I am _____

I am _____

I am _____

I _____

I _____

I _____

I _____

I _____

"Get un-stuck by just getting going." - #LaGringa

Day 352: Today's Date: ___/___/____

I am _____

I am _____

I am _____

I am _____

I am _____

I am _____

I am _____

I am _____

I am _____

I am _____

I am _____

I am _____

I am _____

I am _____

I am _____

I am _____

I _____

I _____

I _____

I _____

I _____

"Be completely transparent all the time." - #LaGringa

Day 353: Today's Date: ___/___/____

I am _____

I am _____

I am _____

I am _____

I am _____

I am _____

I am _____

I am _____

I am _____

I am _____

I am _____

I am _____

I am _____

I am _____

I am _____

I _____

I _____

I _____

I _____

I _____

"Embrace being weird." - #LaGringa

Day 354: Today's Date: ___/___/____

I am _____

I am _____

I am _____

I am _____

I am _____

I am _____

I am _____

I am _____

I am _____

I am _____

I am _____

I am _____

I am _____

I am _____

I am _____

I _____

I _____

I _____

I _____

I _____

"Today, get to know yourself." - #LaGringa

Day 355: Today's Date: ___/___/____

I am _____

I am _____

I am _____

I am _____

I am _____

I am _____

I am _____

I am _____

I am _____

I am _____

I am _____

I am _____

I am _____

I am _____

I am _____

I _____

I _____

I _____

I _____

I _____

"There are 365 days in a year, not 356." - #LaGringa

Day 356: Today's Date: ___/___/____

I am _____

I am _____

I am _____

I am _____

I am _____

I am _____

I am _____

I am _____

I am _____

I am _____

I am _____

I am _____

I am _____

I am _____

I am _____

I _____

I _____

I _____

I _____

I _____

**"Don't allow people who say you are being too self-important to cloud your mind.
You ARE important, and its ok to act like it" - #LaGringa**

Day 357: Today's Date: ___/___/____

I am _____

I am _____

I am _____

I am _____

I am _____

I am _____

I am _____

I am _____

I am _____

I am _____

I am _____

I am _____

I am _____

I am _____

I am _____

I _____

I _____

I _____

I _____

I _____

"#Blessed." - #LaGringa

Day 358: Today's Date: ___/___/___

I am _____

I am _____

I am _____

I am _____

I am _____

I am _____

I am _____

I am _____

I am _____

I am _____

I am _____

I am _____

I am _____

I am _____

I am _____

I _____

I _____

I _____

I _____

I _____

"Learn how to be healthy." - #LaGringa

Day 359: Today's Date: ___/___/____

I am _____

I am _____

I am _____

I am _____

I am _____

I am _____

I am _____

I am _____

I am _____

I am _____

I am _____

I am _____

I am _____

I am _____

I am _____

I _____

I _____

I _____

I _____

I _____

"Would you 10-years ago be proud of the you that you've become?" - #LaGringa

Day 360: Today's Date: ___/___/____

I am _____

I am _____

I am _____

I am _____

I am _____

I am _____

I am _____

I am _____

I am _____

I am _____

I am _____

I am _____

I am _____

I am _____

I am _____

I _____

I _____

I _____

I _____

I _____

Did you order your next copy of I AM: A Life Changing Guide to Creating the Future that you Desire yet???

Purchase yours today on Amazon.com
Or Contact Janine at:

Email: JanineNaomiGrant@icloud.com
Facebook: JanineNaomiGrant
Instagram: @JanineNaomiLive
Twitter: @JanineNaomiLive
LinkedIn: Janine Naomi Grant

"Today is a day that you will change the World." - #LaGringa

Day 361: Today's Date: ___/___/____

I am _____

I am _____

I am _____

I am _____

I am _____

I am _____

I am _____

I am _____

I am _____

I am _____

I am _____

I am _____

I am _____

I am _____

I am _____

I am _____

I _____

I _____

I _____

I _____

I _____

"I believe in you. I care about you. I am confident you will succeed." - #LaGringa

Day 362: Today's Date: ___/___/____

I am _____

I am _____

I am _____

I am _____

I am _____

I am _____

I am _____

I am _____

I am _____

I am _____

I am _____

I am _____

I am _____

I am _____

I am _____

I _____

I _____

I _____

I _____

I _____

"Embrace being weird." - #LaGringa

Day 363: Today's Date: ___/___/____

I am _____

I am _____

I am _____

I am _____

I am _____

I am _____

I am _____

I am _____

I am _____

I am _____

I am _____

I am _____

I am _____

I am _____

I am _____

I _____

I _____

I _____

I _____

I _____

"Thank YOU." - #LaGringa

Day 364: Today's Date: ___/___/____

I am _____

I am _____

I am _____

I am _____

I am _____

I am _____

I am _____

I am _____

I am _____

I am _____

I am _____

I am _____

I am _____

I am _____

I am _____

I _____

I _____

I _____

I _____

I _____

"GRACIAS." - #LaGringa

Day 365: Today's Date: ___/___/____

I am _____

I am _____

I am _____

I am _____

I am _____

I am _____

I am _____

I am _____

I am _____

I am _____

I am _____

I am _____

I am _____

I am _____

I am _____

I am _____

I _____

I _____

I _____

I _____

I _____

"You Are…

Wonderful
Incredible
Loved
Appreciated."

#LaGringa

STOP and fill out this page BEFORE moving forward.

Has this practice been impactful for you in the last year?

(circle one)

YES   No   YES   Maybe   YES

If you circled YES… YAY!!!! Now it is time to pay it forward. What if you could change 10 people's lives today? You can. And you have been!!!! You have impacted 15 people so far by sharing this book – GET IT!!!!! Whether you see it right now or not I am confident you had a MAJOR impact in their life. Now YOU have the power to change MORE people's lives simply by sharing this book with them!!!! It is time to impact the WORLD, again.

Who are 10 people in your life that you think could benefit from this practice?
1. YOURSELF – Did you order your new copy yet? _____
2. _____
3. _____
4. _____
5. _____
6. _____
7. _____
8. _____
9. _____
10. _____

What can you do to make sure that they get a new copy of this journal in the next 10 days?
    Meet up for coffee and explain to them how much this has impacted you
    Send them a link to purchase the book on Amazon
    Post it on Social media and tag them
    Send them a text message about how impactful it has been for you
    Hand write a letter to them about the impact and send it in the mail
    Purchase them a copy as a gift

ABOUT THE AUTHOR

WHO AM I?

I am Janine Naomi Grant.
I am La Gringa.
I am a granddaughter, daughter, sister, and friend.
I am a badass.
I am a future spouse and mother.
I am a loving person.
I am sunshine.
I am a tremendous force for good in the Universe.
I am strong.
I am confident.
I am your friend if you are reading this.
I am impacting the World.
I am an author.
I am an integrated marketing expert.
I am a social media influencer.
I am abundant.
I am an entrepreneur.
I am manifesting my own destiny.
I am fun.
I am beautiful inside and out.
I am a business woman.
I am determined to succeed.
I am absolutely incredible! And so are YOU.

Made in the USA
Middletown, DE
27 June 2017